DIGITAL MARKETING
GROWTH HACKS

The World's Best Digital
Marketers Share Insights on
How They Grow Their Business
with Digital

Ian Cleary, Dave Kerpen, Erik Qualman, Andrea Vahl,
John Jantsch,Viveka von Rosen, Michael Brenner,
Lon Safko, Martin Shervington, Emeric Ernoult,
Brian Massey, Phylis Khare, Andrew Davis and Jamie Turner

Digital Marketing Growth Hacks by Ian Cleary, Dave Kerpen, Erik Qualman, Andrea Vahl, John Jantsch,Viveka von Rosen, Michael Brenner, Lon Safko, Martin Shervington, Emeric Ernoult, Brian Massey, Phylis Khare, Andrew Davis and Jamie Turner

Book design by Maria Soloveya

ISBN: 9781981024896

Contents

Contents

Acknowledgments

The book you see before you is a compilation of the very best ideas from the very best authors in the world on the subjects of social media, digital communications, marketing, and technology.

Many of these authors are New York Times and Amazon #1 best-selling authors and have been major contributors in the development of the industry we call social media.

Many of us have been friends, colleagues, and fellow speakers around the globe for more than a decade. It has always been our hope that someday we would be able to make the time to join forces and share with you our most profound thoughts on today's technologies and give insights into the psychology of human interaction.

We are grateful to you for reading this book and hopefully finding valuable insights that you too may pass along to others. For that, we all say, "Thank you!"

"If I have seen further, it is by standing on the shoulders of giants."

- Sir Isaac Newton, 1675

Introduction to Tools

Tools can do so much for your business. They can save you time, they can make you more productive, and they can make your business look more professional. But they can also waste your time as you learn how to use them and ultimately, they may not be the right tool for you.

Ian Cleary has made technology tools his business by reviewing all types of technology tools on his blog RazorSocial. In this chapter, he shares his very best technology tools so you don't have to do all the time-wasting searching yourself.

Marketing Technology Tools

Ian Cleary

What are the hottest marketing tools you should be using?

The following outlines a range of tools that we'd highly recommend for your digital marketing. If you don't have a good strategy in place tools won't help you. But with the right strategy tools can help make you more efficient and effective.

Marketing Automation

Marketing automation *(https://www.razorsocial.com/advanced-marketing-automation/)* is a big growth area and if you haven't invested in a marketing automation tool now is the time to do so. Let's look at some numbers.

In just two years, marketing automation has grown from being a $500 million industry to a $1.2 billion one. It can streamline a lot of key marketing functions, and it's proving itself as a great revenue driver for companies large and small.

Many marketers choose to invest in MA because it gives them the ability to generate more and better-quality leads. Research shows that companies that use marketing automation to generate leads have a 53% higher conversion rate on average. And this is just one of the many areas where marketing automation can super-charge your results.

We use Ontraport for most of our marketing automation needs. We also like to use Zapier which links hundreds of apps and helps us automate repetitive tasks. SalesManago *(https://www.salesmanago.com/info/home.htm?timeZoneId=CET)* is an automation platform we have recently tested out, and this is the one to watch!

Ontraport

Ontraport *(www.razorsocial.com/go/ontraport/)* is loaded with powerful features that let you automate a variety of marketing tasks, and it comes with a built-in CRM tool.

You can use it to automate your email campaigns, send automated SMS messages to your email subscribers, quickly create and test email capture landing pages, or for functions like lead scoring and routing, task management, and more.

This all-in-one solution also offers rich shopping cart functionality, allowing you to quickly set up and customize your shopping cart, show upsell offers or set up automated abandoned cart emails.

Zapier

Zapier *(https://www.razorsocial.com/zapier-automation/)* is a great tool for automating your marketing tasks. It connects different

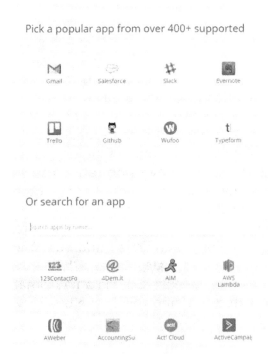

online services and lets you automate the tasks between them by using Triggers and Actions.

An example of zap can be - When I receive a new email (the trigger) in Gmail, send me an SMS message (the action).

You can connect up to 9 social networks and other online services (called 'apps') to your account. Currently, there are 500+ apps and services you can choose from.

You can use pre-made zaps and personalize how they work for you, or you can set up a new zap from scratch.

They recently added multi-step zaps where you can set up a chain of automation. For example, automatically send a tweet based on a trigger, and then automatically store that tweet in a Word document.

Analytics and Testing

The best thing about online marketing is that you can have a complete understanding of which marketing tactics are bringing results and which are a waste of your time and resources.

Testing, analytics, and optimization of your marketing activities are critical to success. Thankfully, there are some great tools out there to help you with that.

Google Analytics

If we had to suggest only one tool to help you track the effectiveness of your campaigns, as well as the performance of your website, it would be Google Analytics.

This tool is completely free to use and it gives you insights into everything that happens on your website – from visitor behavior and characteristics, traffic sources, page views and bounce rates, to conversions and referrals.

Google Analytics *(https://www.razorsocial.com/google-analytics-terms/)* also integrates with AdWords allowing you to measure and optimize your campaigns. Other useful features include sentiment monitoring and trending topics analytics, mobile app analytics, event tracking, and much more.

Don't leave home without Google Analytics! It's an essential tool to measure and optimize the performance of your digital marketing.

Visual Website Optimizer

Visual Website Optimizer *(https://vwo.com/)* is a tool for performing A/B and multivariate testing. Unlike some other tools that entail a steep learning curve, it is quite easy to use – you can set up and run tests in minutes with little or no help from IT. This means you can run tests without having to make changes to the underlying code of the page.

To use the tool for A/B testing *(https://blog.bufferapp.com/how-buffer-ab-tests),* you just copy-paste a code snippet in your website once and you can create unlimited tests anywhere on your website. VWO has a drag and drop interface allowing you to easily change and update any element of the page.

VWO lets you track revenue, signups, clicks, engagement, or any other conversion goal.

Hotjar

Hotjar *(https://www.hotjar.com/)* is a tool that offers some interesting metrics that you cannot get from Google Analytics. It shows the behavior of your website visitors via heatmaps, clickmaps, scrollmaps, and visitor recordings.

Visitor recordings is a very useful feature. It lets you see how visitors behave on your website, capturing their clicks, taps and mouse movements.

Hotjar also lets you analyze your funnel to find opportunities for improvement. Other useful features include Form Analysis for improving form completion rates, Feedback Polls to help you better understand the needs and wants of your website visitors, and Surveys to help you collect feedback from your visitors via web links or emails.

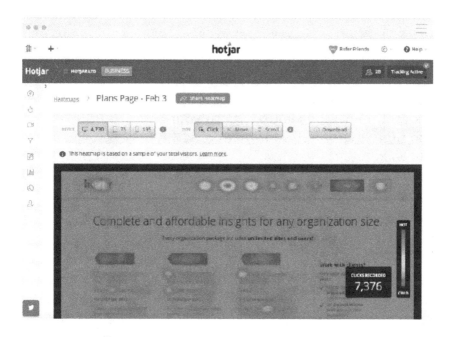

Brand24

Brand24 *(www.razorsocial.com/go/brand24aff/)* is a social media monitoring tool that allows you to track mentions about your brand, or your competition, across social media channels, blogs, forums, photo sites, etc.

To start using the tool you need to set up the keywords you want to monitor. You can also add negative keywords and limit the sites you want

to monitor. Then you can track mentions through Brand24 apps for iPhone and Android, or through email alerts.

The tool also allows you to create a colorful status report, export your report to Excel, or automatically produce an infographic-style report. Sentiment analysis is also available, so you can filter by positive, negative or neutral mentions.

Talkwalker Alerts

Talkwalker is a very powerful social media analytics tool *(https://www.talkwalker.com/)* but it also provides a free alternative to Google Alerts. It monitors news, blogs, and discussions for keywords that you specify.

The tool then sends you alerts to your email or RSS feed reader each time it finds relevant mentions.

Talkwalker Alerts *(https://www.talkwalker.com/alerts)* is free and it comes with limited functionality. However, the main Talkwalker platform is extremely comprehensive and the pricing starts at $500. Although this is not suitable for a small business, it's a good solution for larger businesses.

Content Marketing

Here's a list of content marketing tools that we use and that can help you get started creating a great content marketing program:

BuzzSumo

BuzzSumo *(http://buzzsumo.com/)* is a tool for analyzing what content performs best for any topic related to your business or niche. You can enter a keyword and find the most shared content related to that keyword. It shows not only the number of shares but also a list of the most influential people that shared the content.

BuzzSumo is great for discovering the most popular/shareable content for your website or your competitors' websites. It has a nice set of filters so you can choose to see results based on date, type of content, or by language or country.

Another useful capability of BuzzSumo is that it lets you see backlinks on any piece of content with additional information about the sites that linked to it, such as Domain Authority, the number of followers, etc.

Identifying popular content on your site and your competitors' sites is really useful because it shows you what type of content you should be producing and sharing more of.

Feedly

Feedly *(https://feedly.com/i/welcome)* is an excellent tool that allows you to collect and read content from all your favorite industry blogs or news sites in one place. You can subscribe to as many RSS feeds as you like, and you can organize the content into relevant categories.

Feedly is the easiest way to curate content from your favorite publications for social sharing. You can choose to save posts or share them on your social accounts directly from the Feedly interface.

It is available both as Web and mobile application (Android and iOS.)

SEMrush

SEMrush *(https://www.semrush.com/)* is a great tool for driving more traffic to your website. It analyzes Google organic and paid search results and produces a detailed analysis to help you evaluate your site and the sites of your competition.

For example, you can analyze the keywords your competitor is ranking for, pull their backlinks, view estimated organic traffic they are getting, and conduct a complete competitive analysis.

Overall, this is a great tool for competitor research and we use it on a regular basis. You can start with a free version which offers some limited but useful analytics features, and later decide if you want to upgrade to a paid version.

KWFinder

KWFinder *(https://kwfinder.com/)* is a keyword research tool that will help you identify the best long tail keywords to target. It's also

an excellent Google Keyword Planner *(https://www.razorsocial.com/ google-keyword-planner/)* alternative as it provides exact monthly search volumes along with many other useful metrics.

When entering your keywords, you can select a specific language, and even restrict your results to a particular country or city. The tool will return tons of related long tail keywords with search volume, CPC and difficulty, as well as SERP results with some valuable SEO metrics.

SEOmonitor

SEOmonitor *(https://www.seomonitor.com/)* is a powerful SEO tool that provides a great deal of useful information, allowing you to examine your overall SEO performance.

It allows you to analyze organic traffic data and it segments the organic visits in branded and non-branded. There is a Visibility Score tool that calculates how many people actually see your website in Google results, and it does this by considering the total of searches for a list of most relevant keywords.

You can use SEOmonitor to perform keyword research and look at the stats such as Keyword Opportunity, Difficulty, Bounce rates & CPC and Revenue Forecasts.

Social Warfare

Social Warfare *(https://warfareplugins.com/)* is a very popular social sharing WordPress plugin. You can customize the look of your social share buttons with over 5,000 potential style combinations to fit your website.

There is a Custom Tweets feature that lets you specify a unique message to share on Twitter. You can also upload a Pinterest-specific image and description, add ClickToTweet messages, and choose if, and when, you display share counts on the button.

Google Keyword Planner

Google Keyword Planner *(https://www.razorsocial.com/google-keyword-planner/)* is a free keyword research tool accessible through a Google AdWords account only. It can help you find a wide range of keywords and related data that you can use for content marketing and SEO, or for your AdWords campaigns.

The tool has some limitations - it enables you to only view exact matches on keywords you are researching ('broad match' is not available), plus you can view average searches for keywords but you can't distinguish between devices.

Main capabilities are:

- Search for keyword ideas
- Enter or upload keywords to see how they perform
- Create multiple keyword lists

The Google Keyword Planner provides some good keyword research options. You do need a Google AdWords account but that doesn't force you to advertise.

BuzzStream

BuzzStream *(www.razorsocial.com/go/buzzstream/)* is a great tool for tracking and managing your influencer outreach efforts. Even though this tool offers some functionality to identify relevant influencers and blogs, its main purpose is to help you manage your email outreach program.

You can create email templates for outreach and track all communications through BuzzStream. Additionally, if you set up the Twitter/email address BuzzStream will track any @mentions or direct messages on Twitter or email communications, and add this to your profile.

If you want to promote your content through outreach, this is an excellent tool to manage your outreach campaigns and track results.

Pocket

Pocket *(https://getpocket.com/)* is the best way to save articles, videos and links from the web or mobile apps to view at any time. You can open the Pocket app (iOS, Android, Mac and Windows apps available) and view something you've already saved even if you're offline.

The nice thing about Pocket is that you can read articles right within the app, without having to go back to the original website. You can also sync the content with your Kobo eReader.

The app keeps your favorite resources neatly organized by using tags. It also allows you to share links via Buffer, Facebook, Twitter and Email.

Bonus: **Download a PDF list of all the tools in the article.**
Get the guide now! *(https://www.razorsocial.com/resources/market-ing-tools/)*

Scoop.it

Scoop.it *(https://www.scoop.it/)* is an incredible content curation platform that allows you to easily find and share unique, relevant content to your social networks, website or blog.

Scoop.it allows you to find content based on the keywords you specify. You can then curate the content, include your commentary and publish to your own topic page.

The platform is quite useful if you don't have time to write content for your website or blog, as it allows you to embed content in your website.

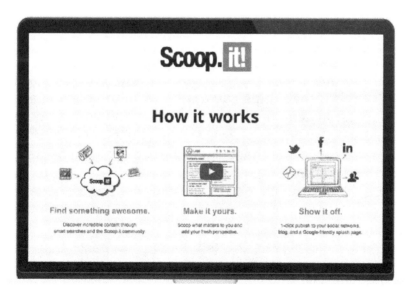

Ahrefs

Ahrefs *(www.razorsocial.com/go/ahrefs/)* is a tool that lets you perform competitive backlinks analysis. It is really useful for finding out the quality links your competition is getting, but also for analyzing your own links. You can identify which pages on your website or blog are the most popular, e.g. have the best links.

This tool also makes it very easy to find most popular content on the web for any topic related to your business. The popularity of content is measured by backlinks, organic traffic, and social shares.

Page	Ahrefs Rank	8+			f	Backlinks	Nofollow
www.socialmediatoday.com/	15	89,743	272	488	1,500	1,993	185
www.socialmediatoday.com/SMC/	15	0	14	9	41	219	1
www.socialmediatoday.com/pamdyer/1595451/5-content-curation-infographics	14	121	354	18	62	153	152
www.socialmediatoday.com/content/gadbad-watch-fault-our-stars-online-free-megashare	20	0	0	0	0	74	74
www.socialmediatoday.com/content/when-should-you-post-your-social-media-content-there-magic-time	14	8	126	2	6	68	68

Ahrefs provides great functionality to help you focus your link building efforts.

Yoast SEO

Yoast SEO *(https://yoast.com/wordpress/plugins/seo/)* is a WordPress SEO plugin that helps you easily optimize your website to perform better in search results. It helps you keep your content in line with SEO best practices by providing built-in content analysis, management of Meta tags and keywords, rich snippets, social features, and more.

Yoast SEO lets you choose a focus keyword and then analyzes the content of your post against that keyword, and gives it an SEO score along with recommendations for improvement.

If you're on WordPress, this is probably the best plugin for optimizing your content for Google.

Influencer Marketing

There are many tools that can help you identify, connect and build relationships with relevant influencers. Following are the tools we use to get the most out of our influencer marketing *(https://blog.kissmetrics.com/guide-to-influencer-targeting/)* campaigns:

GroupHigh

GroupHigh *(https://www.grouphigh.com/)* is a blogger outreach tool with a database of over 13 million categorized blogs you can search through. The information returned for each blog is very comprehensive – it includes 40 metrics which gives you a ton of valuable information to help you create your shortlist of blogs.

It allows you to track your outreach campaigns and report on the results. The tool also records outreach activity history for any particular blog.

GroupHigh is a really useful blogger research tool with the only downside being a pretty high price tag. Make sure you can get sufficient benefit from it so you can justify the investment.

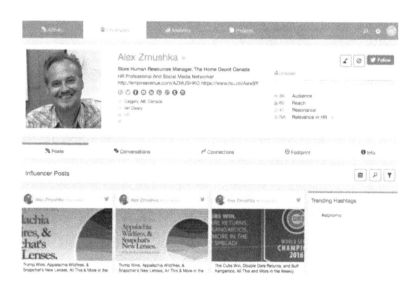

Traackr

Traackr *(http://www.traackr.com/)* is a complete influencer management platform that lets you find influencers and manage all communication with them.

It shows the social media profiles of the influencer, blog posts, conversations, connections, footprint or the size of the profile across multiple sites, and more.

Traackr is great for monitoring the relationship status so you know what stage you are at with each influencer.

Klear

Klear *(https://klear.com/)* is a social intelligence platform that analyzes and reports on the social followings of users broken down into over 60,000 categories with over 500 million profiles and 5 years of historical data. This is also a good tool for identifying influencers.

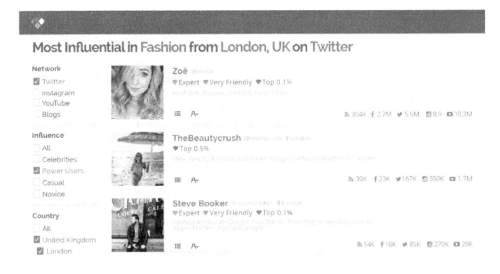

Social Media

Managing social media can be very time-consuming, so we're going to give you a list of tools to take your social media marketing, monitoring, publishing, and analytics to another level.

AdEspresso

AdEspresso *(www.razorsocial.com/go/adespresso/)* is a tool for creating Facebook Ads that has the power of Power Editor but makes the process of creating ads much simpler.

The tool lets you create campaigns quickly by specifying the campaign name and targeting details. When creating your ads with AdEspresso, you can easily set up and test different variations of your ad. The tool can automatically test different images, headlines, ad copy, etc.

You then need to publish the ad directly to Facebook and, once approved, you'll start to see results.

AgoraPulse

AgoraPulse *(www.razorsocial.com/go/agorapulse/)* is a social media management tool which supports all the major social networks, including Facebook, Twitter, Instagram, Google+, and LinkedIn. It allows you to manage social media messages, schedule and share posts, and measure all your activities.

AgoraPulse also includes a suite of apps for building engagement with your followers and fans. You can use them to run competitions, quizzes, sweepstakes, etc.

Detailed performance analytics report is also available for you to download and customize.

Meet Edgar

Meet Edgar *(https://meetedgar.com/)* is a tool for automating and scheduling your social media updates. It allows you to quickly and easily build a library of content to automatically re-share on Facebook, LinkedIn and Twitter.

When building your library, you will first need to specify content categories. There is a default set of categories you can use, but you can also create new categories.

After you've created your categories, you can connect multiple social accounts, set a schedule for each, and then let Edgar take over.

Edgar will keep sending out the content from your queues at the times you have specified. When it gets through the content in a queue, it will start resending it.

Rival IQ

Rival IQ *(https://www.rivaliq.com/)* is a competitive landscape tool. You set up all the competitors you want to track, and then moni-

tor analytics to see how your marketing compares to the competition.

You can compare your performance against your peers across social media, SEO keywords, and website content. Rival IQ lets you monitor things like your competitors' follower growth, their best content, the volume of mentions, the organic traffic they get, etc.

Rival IQ is useful if you want to track multiple competitors to find out their strengths and weaknesses, their position online, and more.

Social Quant

Social Quant *(www.razorsocial.com/go/socialquant-2/)* is a tool that automatically increases the number of your Twitter followers. It is fairly simple to use and there is a free trial available so you can check the inner workings of the tool.

You can create a free account with your Twitter details, and then answer a few questions about who you want to connect with.

Next, you'll input several keywords that are relevant to your audience and Social Quant will start searching and adding new relevant followers to your Twitter account.

TweetChat

TweetChat *(http://tweetchat.com/)* provides some useful functionality to help you manage your Twitter chats. It allows you to monitor and interact with a conversation filtered by a hashtag.

TweetChat allows you to pause a conversation to give you a chance to respond, block or highlight people in a stream, and remove retweets within a stream.

There is also a neat functionality called FavePages that displays all your favorite tweets and categorizes them by date and hashtag.

We use this tool for Twitter chats because it contains the necessary functionality and is easy to use.

TweetBinder

TweetBinder *(https://www.tweetbinder.com/)* is a really useful application for researching hashtags on Twitter and Instagram.

When you search for a hashtag, the tool will return some general stats of the hashtag such as its reach, interaction in terms of likes and comments, users rankings or the people who shared content (most active, popular), and more.

If you want to see how often people are using a hashtag, the influencers sharing it, when it's used etc., this is a useful app.

Audiense

Audiense *(https://audiense.com/)* is a tool for getting more value from Twitter – it provides deep insight into your audiences to help you increase your following and engagement on your Twitter account.

It lets you target new followers based on a number of filters you define. It also analyzes your existing followers to suggest best times to tweet for increased reach and engagement.

Audiense includes a tool for creating highly-targeted Twitter ad campaigns. It gives you a detailed overview of your audience's interests through a feature called Community Insights. There is also a benchmarking feature that lets you compare the performance of your account with similar accounts in your industry.

Schedugr.am

Schedugr.am *(https://schedugr.am/)* is a tool for scheduling on Instagram. It supports multiple accounts and lets you schedule video or imagery. When content is sent out, it is stored so you can easily re-share on a regular basis.

You can add multiple users to schedule posts for your Instagram accounts, and see who has scheduled what.

Landing page tools

LeadPages

LeadPages *(www.razorsocial.com/go/leadpages/)* is a very popular landing page builder that is also simple to use, so you can create high converting landing pages in minutes.

You can choose from a suite of 65 mobile-optimized templates that are proven to convert well. These templates cover a variety of scenarios, including pages for downloading an eBook, signing up for a webinar, etc.

You can easily set up split testing and measure conversion on each page.

It provides integration with a variety of email marketing and marketing automation providers, including Aweber, MailChimp, Constant Contact, Ontraport, Infusionsoft, GetResponse, and many others.

Payment Collection

ThriveCart

ThriveCart *(https://thrivecart.com)* is a popular shopping cart platform that you can use to quickly create cart pages with professionally designed templates.

It allows you to create 1-click upsells, build funnels, perform A/B tests, and much more. ThriveCart also supports integration with marketing automation tools such as Infusionsoft.

Stripe

Stripe *(https://stripe.com/)* is one of the simplest payment processors to set up. We use ThriveCart for creating our checkout pages, and Stripe for collecting the fees.

Email Marketing

Our marketing automation tool (Ontraport) handles all our email communications, but we love to use OptinMonster to generate our subscribers.

OptinMonster

OptinMonster is a WordPress popup plugin for capturing email addressed and growing your subscriber list. There is a wide range of templates available and the setup is very simple. Split testing is available on all op-tins and it's easy to test out.

If you're looking to grow your email subscribers, we highly recommend trying out this tool.

OutreachPlus

If you want to do cold email marketing outreach OutreachPlus *(www.outreachplus.com)* provides great functionality to save you time and improve your conversion rate. This includes automated sequences, proven to convert templates, a prospect database to help with future campaigns and much more.

Visual Marketing

Having the right visual marketing tools at your disposal will help you create compelling visuals on a consistent basis – even if you are a non-designer. Strong visual *(https://www.socialmediaexaminer.com/4-ways-visual-content-improves-social-media-results/)* content is necessary if you want to better tell stories and keep your audiences engaged in a more impressionable way. It is also one of the best ways to stand out from your competition.

Canva

Canva is a web-based tool that lets you create stunning visuals for your blogs and social media. Canva offers pre-sized social media images for various platforms, and it is also a great tool for creating images for marketing materials, presentations, ads, info-graphics, etc.

There's no need to worry if design is not your strong suit – drag and drop editing makes image creation very easy. You can create your image from scratch or choose from a wide variety of background images, stock photos, and designs that Canva pro-vides.

If you choose to use your own photos, you can upload them from your computer, Facebook, or Google Drive.

Canva simplifies the design process and is perfect for market-ers who have the need to consistently create visuals to accompa-ny their social media updates and blog post.

Adobe Spark

Spark *(https://spark.adobe.com/home/)* is a free graphic design app that lets you create social graphics, web stories, and animat-ed videos.

It consists of three main tools — Post, Page, and Video.

Spark Post lets you create images with text overlays. It's easy to use and you can change font style, colors, layouts and image size.

Spark Page generates Web page stories from your images, text and video and allows you to choose from a variety of curated designs. You can use a feature called GlideShow to add motion effect to text and images on your page.

Spark Video lets you pick a template for your story and then combine text, icons, images, animations, effects, and audio to create your video.

WordSwag

WordSwag *(http://wordswag.co/)* lets you create beautiful graphics for Instagram, Twitter, Facebook, Tumblr, and your blog.

It has an amazing set of image and typography templates and it lets you create great looking images with text overlay. You can upload photos from your camera roll, take photos from within the app, or choose from a gallery of available images and backgrounds.

Video Marketing and Live Streaming

There's no better way to bring your digital stories to life than video – both recorded and live! There are many tools out there that you can use to manage your YouTube channel, create animated videos, or to host a live show. The ones we recommend here are either low cost or free and also quite easy to use.

TubeBuddy

TubeBuddy *(https://www.tubebuddy.com/)* is a browser extension aimed at helping YouTube creators optimize and grow their channels. It's packed with some amazing functionality that will help you save time, optimize your videos, and keep your audience engaged.

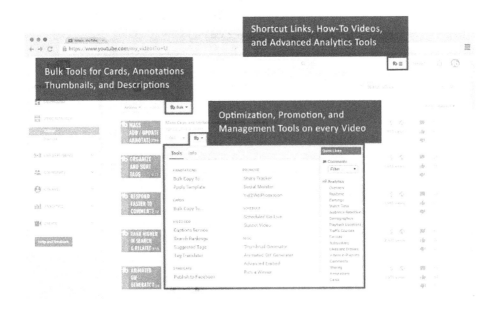

TubeBuddy offers a set of tools that you can use straight from the YouTube's website. You can use the Bulk Processing tools to automate processes such as adding annotations, cards, or descriptions to multiple videos. This can save you A LOT of time!

It also offers a number of productivity tools, such as direct

Facebook uploads and custom thumbnail generator. TubeBuddy also comes with a set of very useful SEO tools that can help you improve your video rankings in YouTube search.

In addition, if you want to benchmark your channel's performance against the competition, perform subscriber outreach, or discover the best time to publish videos for your audience – they've got you covered!

You can start using TubeBuddy for free or go with one of their premium plans *(https://www.tubebuddy.com/pricing)* for a more feature-rich experience.

GoAnimate

GoAnimate *(www.razorsocial.com/go/goanimate/)* is an online, DIY video animation tool. It lets you create your own animated videos using templates, characters, voice recordings etc.

GoAnimate allows you to pick from a library of characters, props and scenes and then build your video up scene by scene with a drag and drop editor. You can also choose a voice you want to add to your animation or record your own voice.

There's an option to add background music to your scenes. This can be your own music or you can choose it from a library.

When you're finished, you can export high-definition videos that you can then embed on your blog or upload to YouTube.

GoAnimate is a cost-effective, easy-to-use tool and it's also a lot of fun to play with.

OBS

OBS *(https://obsproject.com/)* is a tool for live streaming that allows you to live stream to Facebook Live (other platforms are supported also.) What's great about it is that it's free (!), but also the extra functionality you can have with it.

For example, you can display your logo while you're live streaming or a nice banner image. You can easily swap between live and recorded videos, and much more.

Wirecast

Wirecast *(https://www.telestream.net/wirecast/overview.htm)* is a tool for live streaming to Facebook and other platforms. It has more functionality that OBS but it's a paid for tool.

Live Streaming Equipment

Read this post on live streaming to find out about the tools to use (e.g. microphones, mixers, etc.) – Live streaming tools *(https://www.razorsocial.com/tools-and-tips-for-going-live-on-facebook/)*.

ScreenFlow

ScreenFlow is a great tool for creating, editing, and producing videos on your MAC. If you're on a PC - use Camtasia.

You can do basic editing very easily and pick up the advanced stuff over time.

Ripl

Ripl *(https://www.ripl.com/)* allows you to create animated social media posts from a series of images using one of their templates. You can also add sound to the video – upload your own music or choose from the Ripl music library.

Website tools

Tawk.to

Tawk.to *(https://www.tawk.to/)* is a free app that lets you monitor and chat with your website visitors in real-time and from any device.

Setup is quite simple – just copy a simple line of JavaScript into the HTML of your website and the chat widget will immediately start working.

You can customize the look of the app on your website by changing the color of the chat pop-up and the text in it. Tawk.to integrates with WordPress, Joomla, Magento, etc.

GTmetrix Speed Test

GTmetrix *(https://gtmetrix.com/)* is a free tool that analyzes your website's speed by checking both PageSpeed and YSlow metrics. It also suggests dozens of different ways to improve your website speed performance.

The basic functionality of GTMetrix is free and you can analyze the speed of your website right from the service's homepage.

The results overview shows you the browser and location used for testing, PageSpeed and YSlow scores, page load time, the number of requests and total page size.

Summary

Without a good strategy, tools will not help, but with the right strategy....

About Ian Cleary

Ian Cleary is founder of RazorSocial and is a passionate content marketer, professional speaker and award winning blogger. He writes for Forbes and Entrepreneur.com and spoke recently at Content Marketing World, MarTech and Social Media Marketing world. He believes that technology can give you the edge that you need in today's competitive market.

Introduction to Facebook Ads

Facebook Ads have gotten more complex since they have been introduced, but they can be a powerful way to reach your ideal customer and grow your business. However, if you aren't using them right, you can waste a lot of money.

In this chapter, Andrea Vahl shares how to really use Facebook Ads effectively. Andrea is the co-author of Facebook Marketing All-in-One for Dummies and runs Facebook ad campaigns for all types of businesses.

How Facebook Ads Can Bring You Highly Targeted Leads And Sales

Andrea Vahl

Facebook is the largest social network on the web, but many business owners and marketers still don't know how to take advantage of all Facebook has to offer. To complicate matters, Facebook continually changes their layout and their News Feed algorithm to make it a moving target for marketers. Just when you get comfortable with what is working, it shifts.

Some people talk about metrics such as the perfect time to post, the perfect length of post, the perfect way to post a link. But none of that matters as much as posting content that your audience cares about.

Yes, there are strategies that work better on Facebook in terms of getting more visibility (like Facebook Live video), and when you focus on providing good content consistently your audience will make sure they go out of their way to find you.

There is no doubt that Facebook is increasingly becoming a "pay-to-play" platform with Pages getting less exposure in the News Feed than they have in the past. But that should not scare marketers away. In fact, I see it as an amazing opportunity to use Facebook to reach your perfect audience. Facebook is one the cheapest and best places to advertise online today.

But the big question everyone has is: How do I get Facebook Ads to work for me?

The answer lies in the goals you have for your Facebook Ads. Many people think that they should be able to sell their products and services right from a Facebook Ad. And in that case, I say that Facebook Ads rarely work unless you have your targeting set right and are only targeting your warm market (people who know you, who have visited your website, or are on your e-mail list.)

Facebook Ads shine when you have one of these **4 goals:**

- Building your e-mail list by offering something good for free.
- Sending traffic to your website so that people can read a blog post or get a freebie.
- Getting engagement from your current Facebook community.

Retargeting your warm audience (website visitors or email subscribers) with a special offer.

When you really look at it, these three goals are very similar. **We are using Facebook Ads to connect to targeted Facebook users and eventually get them to our e-mail list.** When we are doing things like boosted post to our own Fans, each post should have the ulterior motive of getting them to our website where they get to know us more and get on our e-mail list (if they aren't already.)

Before You Start Advertising on Facebook

Before you dive into Facebook Ads you will need to have a few key elements:

- **Facebook Page:** You will need a Page to get your ad in the News Fee which is where it gets the most clicks. It doesn't have to have a lot of Fans, it just needs to represent your business well.
- **E-mail System:** Make sure you are using some e-mail autoresponder such as Aweber, Constant Contact, MailChimp, or Infusionsoft.
- **Special Offer:** This can be a free report, a free webinar, a white paper, free trial or free product. Make sure this is something valuable that people would pay for and that your target audience would find irresistible. Make it highly relevant to your business so that you get quality people who opt-in to this offer.
- **Opt-in Page:** This can be a special page on your website where you showcase this offer. Try to make it free of distrac-

tions such as other navigation on your site or links that they might click. You can use a WordPress Plugin such as Optimize Press or a special tool like LeadPages to help you create something quickly.

- **Thank You Page:** This will be a separate page on your website where you let them know that they have successfully opted in. You could also deliver the content there that they requested. It's important to have a Thank You page because this will be how you measure your conversions.
- **Facebook Pixel Installed on your Website:** You need to have the Facebook Pixel installed so that you can track your traffic from your Facebook Ads. Read my post about how to install it and set it up here *(www.andreavahl.com/facebook/facebookadspixel.php)*.

Once you have everything set up, you can use Facebook Ads to drive qualified traffic to the Opt-in Page. Use the Detailed Targeting in Facebook Ads to target the perfect demographic and interests of your ideal client. You can even target the Fans of other Pages using the Detailed Targeting field.

Facebook Ads Targeting

The keywords and targeting you choose for your Facebook Ad is going to make the biggest difference in how successful your ads are. The Facebook Ad targeting system is much more robust than people realize due to 3rd party data that is collected and matched to Facebook users (everything we do is being tracked on the web, right?)

Here are just a few things you can target by:

- Age, location (city, zip code, state, or country), gender.
- Education, job titles, income, parents (by age range of children), relationship status.
- Behaviors such as online purchasing, car ownership, device usage, and more.
- General interest keywords or the fans of specific Facebook Pages.

Your website visitors, people who have watch a video of yours, your email subscribers, people who have purchased your products, people who have interacted with your Facebook Page.

- Lookalike audiences (people who are similar to people who have visited your website or purchased your products.)

Can you see how powerful targeting can be?

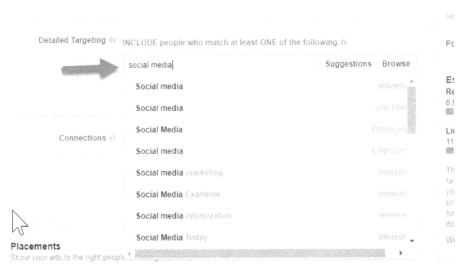

Some of the more general keywords and demographics are targeted in the Detailed Targeting area of the Facebook Ad setup.

Facebook Ads for Leads

To get a lead you need something valuable to give away to entice someone to give you their email address or contact information. Here are some ideas for things you can offer:

- **Exclusive Coupon:** Great for local businesses that need that foot traffic.
- **Free Report or Whitepaper:** This doesn't have to be very long, it just needs to offer valuable tips that your potential customer is interested in and that relate directly to your business.

- **Webinar or Teleseminar:** Offer a short class or free call – this could be live or pre-recorded.
- **Contests:** Use these throughout the year to give away something directly related to your business.
- **E-course:** Use a set of e-mails to teach some lessons. Use your automated e-mail system to deliver the e-mails – one a day for 10 days, for example.

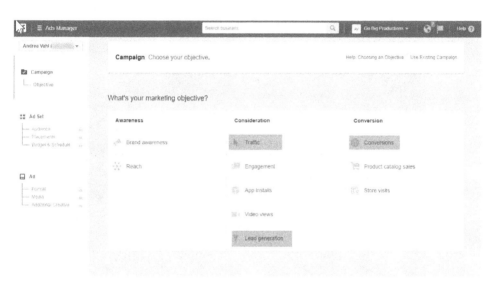

Then you can nurture those connections through an email follow-up sequence or hopefully bring them into your local store with a coupon. Now all you need to do is drive highly targeted traffic to your free offer.

If you have a page where people will opt-in to your offer or free giveaway, then you can send Facebook traffic to that offer by selecting the Traffic or Conversion Objective in Facebook Ads. You will only be able to use the Conversion Objective if you have the Facebook Pixel in place and you have set up the Conversion tracking properly.

You can also select the Lead generation ad but that is a slightly different type of ad where people opt-in to a form that is on Facebook so they don't need to visit your website.

Facebook Ads for Sales

After you have a highly targeted list of e-mail subscribers, use your email follow-up sequence to do your selling for you. Make sure you follow-up with your email list regularly with good content and good offers from your business.

You can also reach the people who were most interested in your offer through Facebook Ads by retargeting the people who have visited that page on your website or the people who signed up for the offer in email.

Retargeting is done through creating Audiences in the Facebook Ads Manager.

Once you create the Audience, then you can use that audience in the targeting area of your ad to only show your sales ad to the people who are going to be most likely to convert – your warm audience. In this example, I show how I can target only the people who have been to the website that sells my Facebook Ads Course. I can also exclude the people who have already purchased the course from seeing my ad.

You can also track the conversions through to a sale with Con-

version tracking in Facebook Ads. But if there is some reason you can't use the Facebook Pixel on your website, you can still track sales from your ad if you use a special coupon code. But that would also mean that you have to give a discount to track in that case. Special, limited-time offers often do better for converting a sale on Facebook.

Special LIMITED promotion until June 1st. Use code SSA10OFF to get 10% off our flagship Sommelier Certificate Course - classes start September 12th. We rarely run promotions - sign up now!

We offer the definitive course for those seeking to advance their careers, expand their wine knowledge and prime their palates, and for passionate wine enthusiasts who desire a career change. Get more information and sign up here: https://sommeliersocietyofamerica.org/

Limited Promotion: The Sommelier Certificate Course Sign up by June 1st

Sommelier Certificate Course - Registration is Open

Each class features at least eight hand selected unique wines, tasting more than 140 wines. Our Chairman, in consultation with the instructors selects exceptional wines to represent each highlighted region. Network while learning.

SOMMELIERSOCIETYOFAMERICA.ORG   Sign Up

36   8 Comments 2 Shares

Facebook Ads Results

With the Facebook Pixel, you will use Conversion tracking to track exactly how much each lead costs you. So now you can run different ads and see which one will give you the best cost per conversion. Start by testing different demographics, then split test different images and copy in your ad. Run reports to see which ads performed the best so that you get the lowest cost per lead.

The outlined column is the cost-per-website conversion and I can sort from lowest to highest to see which ads performed the best in terms of conversions.

How Facebook Ads Have Worked for Me

Social media has been the secret to my success because social media was the main reason I got offered the book deal for Facebook Marketing All-in-One for Dummies. I started building my audience by providing good content on my blog and using my "alter-ego" Grandma Mary, Social Media Edutainer, to deliver fun tutorials. As I did this I connected with Phyllis Khare (now my co-author and also a contributor to this book) on social media.

I grew my blog and my following and I continued to establish authority around Facebook Marketing. Phyllis was in the process of talking with Wiley, the publisher of the Dummies series books and they wanted her to bring in someone with a large following as a co-author. Because of our relationship and my authority on the subject, she thought of me first. So you never know where your connections can lead. We are in an amazing time right now where social media can grow your visibility and your business to places you never thought would be possible.

Now I use Facebook Ads to grow my email list, sell my products such as Social Media Manager School, Social Media Strategy School, and Facebook Advertising Secrets. I also use targeted Facebook Ads to fill local workshops that I've personally run in Denver, London, and Dublin.

But not only that, I run Facebook Ad campaigns for a wide variety of clients such as medical schools, ecommerce products, consultants, therapists, authors, Real Estate agents, dentists, retreats, speakers, and more. Facebook Ads can work for all types of businesses. The most important thing is to be clear on your goal and making sure you are watching the right stats.

Facebook Ads are hard to have a positive return on your investment when you have a low-priced product like a book or a

lower-cost product under $10. I've seen conversion rates as low as $3-6 for a book but it depends on the subject. If you use re-targeting to your warm audience you increase your conversions for your sales ads.

It's hard to give sweeping generalities about Facebook Ads because different techniques work for different niches. It's important to run several types of tests to see what works for you.

Facebook Ads are one of the cheapest, most effective places to advertise online today. And you were worried that Facebook was only good for cat videos!

Action Steps for You:

1) Focus on sending traffic to a freebie that you offer to get people onto your e-mail list.
2) Set up Facebook Website Conversion ads so that you can precisely measure the cost for each opt-in.
3) Look at your reports and analyze which ad performs best for you.
4) Use your e-mail messages to then sell your product or services.

The bottom line is that Facebook Ads work for most businesses when focusing on e-mail opt-ins. Sometimes the cost per conversion can be higher depending on your offering or your niche. By split testing your ads, you can bring that cost down. Give it a try!

About Andrea Vahl

Andrea Vahl is a Social Media Speaker and Consultant who is passionate about helping businesses understand and leverage the power of social media to actually grow their businesses. Andrea is the co-author of *Facebook Marketing All-in-One for Dummies* and was the **Community Manager for Social Media Examiner** for over 2 years.

She was named **50 Favorite Online Influencers of 2014 on Entrepreneur.com, 21 Best Blogs That Will Help You Grow Your Business on Inc.com in 2016,** and **Top 30 Women in Social Media** by Boom Social. She is the **co-founder of Social Media Manager School** and **Social Media Strategy School,** along with Phyllis Khare.

Andrea Vahl's proven ability to make social media marketing easy to understand and implement has directly impacted the bottom line of thousands of companies through her training and one-on-one consulting. Learn more about Andrea and follow her blog at *www.AndreaVahl.com* and get her free Facebook Ads Course at *www.fbadvertisingsecrets.com/freecourse*

Introduction to Blogging on LinkedIn

LinkedIn is more than just a networking site. You can also use it to post longer-form content like a blog post. And often those posts get much more visibility than the blog posts on your own website. Getting in front of the right people with your content can help your business grow.

In this chapter, Dave Kerpen shares his formula for developing the perfect post and getting more visibility. Dave is an internationally-known speaker and best-selling author as well as founder of Likeable Media. He has made visibility part of his business since day one when he funded his entire wedding with sponsorships.

5 Steps to the Perfect Blog Post on LinkedIn

Dave Kerpen

24 million.

That's how many people have viewed my blog content on LinkedIn in the last 3 years. Those 24 million page views led to 600,000+ followers, thousands of sales leads and books sold and more than $1 million of revenue.

I'm super lucky. I've been part of the LinkedIn Influencer program and that's been a huge part of my success. But now, LinkedIn has opened up its publishing platform to its 400 million users. Now, everyone can blog on LinkedIn. These days, with this roadmap, everyone can make money through LinkedIn. Here's exactly how:

1. Think of a great headline

A clear, powerful headline that promises to deliver value to the reader counts for as much as 60% of the overall success of your blog post on LinkedIn, as headlines grab readers' attention in an increasingly crowded landscape. Use the headline to guide your content and deliver what you would tell your best customer.

For example, if you're an accountant, you could try "5 Essential Tax Saving Tips This Year." If you're a small-business growth consultant, you could try "The Secret to Growing Your Business." If you're a recruiter, try "How to Find the Best Talent." Don't worry about giving away your secrets!

2. Find or take a compelling photo

The "hero image" directly beneath the headline counts for about 30% of the overall success of your post on LinkedIn, as people notice images much more than they notice text. A photo of you, or you with one other person that the post will reference, is perfect. Choosing and licensing a photo from a site such as Shutterstock is another option. Don't ever skip the photo.

3. Write a concise post

It depends on what you want to deliver, but typically, 400-600 words is good. Use bold, italics, number and block quotes to add variety to your post. Consider embedding SlideShare presentations and/or videos through LinkedIn's easy-to-use toolbar. Your writing is a reflection of your thinking. If you want to be thought of as a smart thinker, you must become a better writer. If you want to be taken seriously by your manager, colleagues, potential employers, clients and prospects, you must become a better writer. If you want to become a better writer, these are 4 quick tips:

5) **Practice, Practice, Practice:** The best way to get better at anything is to do it repeatedly. The more you write, the better you'll become at writing.
6) **Say it out Loud:** I read all of my articles and books out loud before I publish them, and many of my emails out loud as well. It's great to hear my writing the way others will "hear" it as they read.
7) **Make it More Concise:** People don't have time to read a long email, or memo, or article; so out of respect for your intended audience, practice making your writing short and sweet.
8) **Read:** Besides practicing writing, the number one way to improve your writing skills is to read great work. I know we all have limited time, but truly the best way to become a better writer is to become a better reader.

4. Include two strong "calls to action" at the bottom of your post

Conclude your post with two calls to action for readers: The first should ask readers to comment and give them specific questions to answer related to your post. As comments are a huge driver of virality on LinkedIn, you'll want to solicit comments from your connections and readers. The second call to action is an offer - this is where you'll drive leads, sell books, or solicit app downloads. Drive people to a landing page on your website with a call to action such as "To learn more, click here." Consider a clickable picture here too.

5. Share the post on LinkedIn, Facebook and Twitter

LinkedIn is most obvious network to share your post on, for obvious reasons. Consider sharing it both publicly (with all of your connections) and privately (through messages to key connections.) Consider sharing it with LinkedIn groups you're in, and your company page if you have one.

Don't be afraid to share it up to four times, as your friends and colleagues are logged in at different times through the day and week. Ask your network to share your post with their network.

6. Repeat steps 1 through 5

To obtain the best results, blog consistently, at least once per week, on LinkedIn. Remember, you don't need to reach a million people on LinkedIn in order to make money, you just need to reach a few of the right people. And chances are, no matter what you do, the right people are in your LinkedIn network and your network's network. To reverse-paraphrase the movie *The Social Network*:

> You know what's cooler than reaching 400 million people on LinkedIn? Reaching the right 400 people, with the right message.

Here's to your first post, and to you making lots of money blogging on LinkedIn.

About Dave Kerpen

I'm a father of 2 beautiful girls, Charlotte and Kate, and baby boy Seth, the husband to an amazing business partner, Carrie Kerpen, and friend to many. I'm an entrepreneur, author, and speaker. I've been writing here on LinkedIn for 2 years, so I've amassed a pretty incredible community of 600,000+ people. Welcome to the "family"!

In my day job, I'm the founder and CEO of Likeable Local, a social media software company serving thousands of small businesses, as well as the chairman and cofounder of Likeable Media, an award-winning social media and word-of-mouth marketing agency for big brands.

Following my sponsored wedding, which raised over $100,000 including $20K for charity, my wife Carrie and I started and built theKBuzz (founded in 2007) into Likeable Media, the only 3-time WOMMY Award winner for excellence from the Word of Mouth Marketing Association (WOMMA) and one of the 500 fastest-growing private companies in the US, according to INC Magazine.

As one of Entrepreneur Magazine's top 10 up and coming leaders, I have been featured on the Today Show, CNBC's "On the Money", BBC, ABC World News Tonight, the CBS Early Show, the New York Times, and countless blogs. I have also keynoted at dozens of conferences across the globe including Singapore, Athens, Dubai, San Francisco, Cologne, Toronto, Bangkok, and Mexico City.

My 1st book was a NY Times best-seller - *Likeable Social Media: How to Delight Your Customers, Create an Irresistible Brand, and Be Generally Amazing on Facebook and Other Social Networks* (now in its 2nd edition.) I followed-up *Likeable Social Media* with 2 more books, *Likeable Business & Likeable Leadership*. My newest book, *The Art of People: 11 Simple People Skills That Will Get You Everything You Want,* is out now: http://buyartofpeople.com

Introduction to YouTube

YouTube is one of the biggest search engines on the planet. People are searching for how-to videos every minute of the day and if your video is more "findable" you can get new customers as long as you have the right things in place.

In this chapter, Phyllis Khare shares her strategy for getting leads from YouTube. Phyllis is the author of Social Media Marketing ELearning Kit for Dummies and Facebook Marketing All-in-One for Dummies and has YouTube videos with thousands of views that bring her new leads on auto-pilot every day.

5 Steps to a Solid Lead Using YouTube

Phyllis Khare

Before you start any lead-capturing process using YouTube, you need to start with a few simple steps. The first step might be obvious: you need to have a strategy. Designing a strategy allows you to set a goal. Once you know what your goal is, you can point all your resources and tactics in that direction. Let's go over the basic steps and then drill down into two specific examples, which are being used to great success on YouTube.

1. Design the Strategy by First Setting the Goal

Once you know the goal (for example, growing your email list), you can go on to the next step: figuring out the exact need of that desired audience.

Once you know what they want - and you can find this out through keyword research, Google Analytics, and, my favorite, YouTube long tail research - you'll find that there's something that keeps coming up: questions, or something that they need and continue to ask for. That's where you start.

Once you know what that is, you can create something that satisfies that need. But more on that in a minute. The next step is actually visualizing how the whole process will work:

2. Visualize and Build the Funnel

One of my favorite things to do the go to my gigantic white-board and start drawing a business funnel. Depending on how your brain works this might go left to right, or top to bottom, or inside/outside. The most important thing is to show the flow through time.

If you are new to this idea, think of it this way: "What happens if someone finds my post and clicks on it?" Each step has a box, each box has an arrow, and the next step and everything fits together beautifully. Here's an example of a very simple business funnel flow.

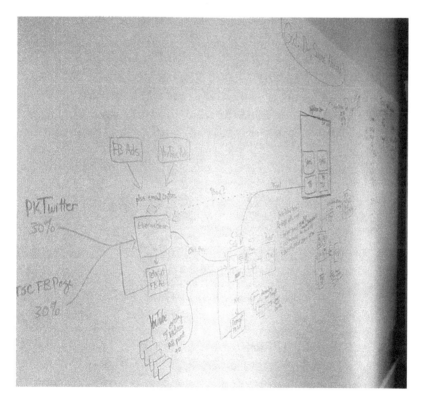

There are many programs available where they create this process for you, automate it, and put it together. I'm sure you've heard of ClickFunnels, ActiveCampaign, and many others that are part of the email capture system itself. Some of these systems can be very pricey and some of them can be very cheap - like my little whiteboard.

The idea is to draw it out and fix any hanging processes or end points. Design all the moving parts on paper (so to speak) until you are sure it all works. Then go to your preferred system to make it real.

3. Create the Attractive Exchange Process

In Step 1, we've figured out what's going to be the answer to your new prospects needs, and we have figured out what type of format that will take. It could be in the form of a video series, it could be in the form of an ebook, it could be in the form of a webinar, or it could be in the form of a phone call. The format is completely dependent on your type of business.

Now I want you to think about the typical email capture system that sits on a website page. It's very boring. Everybody knows how it works. The conversion rate can be very low. So, it might be important right now to think about other options you can use to capturing leads.

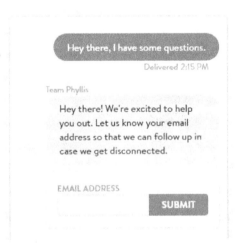

There are some amazing technologies that might help you considerably. One that comes to mind is very easy to test and try out is called Drift. It's one of many live chat programs that you can install on any website, including an e-commerce website like Shopify.

In the process of using that live chat - email can be captured.

In the Drift system, there is an email confirmation process that's built-in and all automatic. You will have text to edit that explains what is done with the email. You can give them options to getting on different lists or you can say this email is for communication purposes only.

Also, if you are very active on Facebook, you can set up Messenger Response Assistant for your page to be an email capture system as you can see in the image. You find this in your Facebook Page Settings → Messaging → Response Assistant.

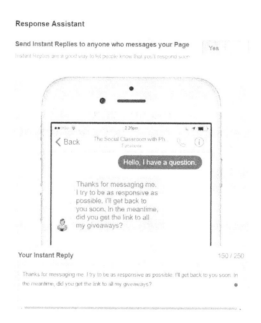

The point being here is don't feel like you are stuck using that tired old email capture box on the right column of your old worn-out website.

When we get to the specific examples from YouTube, you'll see how this is done specifically for a YouTube audience.

The most overlooked thing in this particular step is: making sure that you are capturing the traffic that are visiting this exchange process. You'll need this data so that you can create a custom audience for any advertising you do in the future.

You need to make sure that you have all the codes, tags, or pixels available that will allow you to retarget visitors to whichever site is capturing the email. You need know what's working and what isn't working.

Learning how to track your traffic is a vital step. If you don't want to do this yourself, it is something that can be outsourced to someone on your team. Hopefully. If not, that's a completely different training article!

And the question I can hear rattling around in everyone's head is this...

4. How do I get the Traffic to this Email Capture system?

Really and truly the best way to do this is with advertising. I hate to burst the free organic social media content-generating machine bubble - but if the goal is to add to your email list, you are going to have to put some money into advertising. #reality #runabusinessnotahobby

Now the rule of thumb is: don't advertise to get traffic unless you also have something that is optionally available to purchase through your funnel that can fund the ad costs.

Lots of online marketers have programs that outline this process - my favorite is the one that Mike Dillard promotes. He calls this front-end process a "self-liquidating offer", or SLO. This is a process you see a lot online where you get something for free, and then there's a small upsell in the beginning for something very inexpensive - possibly under $30.

The conversion rate on those $30 offers should completely offset your cost for advertising. Always test this with a tiny budget until you are making money on every ad.

5. Nurture the Interest until you have a Solid Lead or Sale

This is the point in the process where you need to nurture the interest of your email community. The goal is to move them from what they originally got from you, to what you would like them to get from you.

Always provide great service to your community. You will find through time the only things that work are the things that provide great value. This is especially true for online businesses.

When you built your business funnel in Step 2, hopefully you put in some automated email sequences that move someone along in the process of learning to trust you. This is needed for them to take the next step.

Every email that you send to anyone on your list needs to be important and give them quality content, plus a call to action.

Depending on your business the next action could be anything from moving to a higher priced product, to group coaching, private coaching, to one-on-one consulting - whatever that is for your funnel.

And now that you're tracking all of your traffic to your email list, you can track your email list to the next step in the conversion process.

Those are the general business steps to gaining a lead online. Now let's move specifically into how that looks on YouTube:

Examples on YouTube

Step 1 above is to have a strategy so you can set a goal. In this first example the goal is email capture, and the second example is an email capture provided with a free trial or purchase.

Both of these examples have beautifully-designed email capture functions straight from their YouTube channels. And there are several places on the YouTube channel that need to be adjusted to capture leads:

1) Cover Image
2) Description Text
3) Main CTA Link

4) Cards
5) End Credits
6) And the About Section

Example 1 Justin Brown - Primal Video

(https://www.youtube.com/user/EditMyClips0)

Cover image contains CTA and direct link:

He knows his intended audience, has all the correct keywords, the guide is attractive to his audience to solve their problem, and it's easy to click.

Description text contains this CTA and links:

Learn how to make a video intro for YouTube! Step-by-step logo sting and video bumper tutorial. ▶▶FREE GUIDE: The UL-

TIMATE Video Editing Process (https://primalvideo.com/the-pri-mal-video-method/)

Link goes to email capture for a training manual:

From here the process goes along with whatever business funnel he has set up with all the email automation and offers. And by now you know he has some code setup on his email capture page where he can retarget visitors that did not opt-in.

Back on YouTube, he also has Cards, End Credits and CTAs on every video that point to this lead generating item. He also has text in the Channel's About section with a link to this training manual.

Example 2 GrowVeg

(https://www.youtube.com/user/GrowVeg)

Cover image contains direct link:

This business has a garden planning software program. They offer a free trial and a low price purchase.

Their strategy seems to be to get as much traffic as they can to the free trial using YouTube videos.

There is email capture on the free trial interface.

And here's the strategy - every single video has amazing free

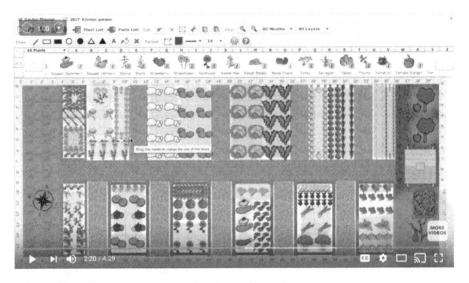

How to Plan a Bigger, Better Garden - Easy Vegetable Garden Planning

content and then maybe 30 seconds of the planner and how it would work doing that particular thing. You get a brief glance into the EASE of using a planner without over-kill in showing it.

They're producing high-quality videos twice a month for their Channel. They are quite savvy with their keywords, title descriptions, thumbnail images, end credits, cards, the whole bit. They've had well over half a million views for their Channel this month, so if your business sells a product, their process is a good one to model.

YouTube's 5 Steps to Gaining a Solid Lead

Here are the five steps (in a nutshell) as they relate specifically to YouTube. Once you have designed your strategy with your main goal selected, and have created the funnel with all the moving parts, THEN you can design and implement these YouTube specific steps.

Step 1: Create a Channel Trailer

Many businesses forget to create a channel trailer. This is the video people will see first if they have not subscribed to your channel. This is what people will see when they find you through search.

Here are some things that need to be in that under 3-minute trailer video:

1) Explain the reason for the Channel in one sentence.
2) Have a direct CTA in the first 30 seconds that solves your audience's main problem - provide an answer to their highest need right away.
3) This video needs to be as professionally-produced as possible.
4) This video also has to convey your personality and the tone of all the videos on your channel right from the get-go.
5) Make sure the descriptive text for this channel trailer has the direct link to your email capture page.

Step 2: Give Great Content and Always have a CTA

Both of the examples I gave follow this rule as they each have incredible content that is completely fueled by the appropriate keywords and they always have a CTA to the next step. The next step could either be to their training manuals or their planning guides or books, or it might be to watch the next video in the series.

Here are some things that need to be in each video:

1) Get in the habit of having a script or at least an outline before you start a video. Know where you are sending people and why they should go there.
2) Depending on your strategy and process you might either tease the link ("at the end of the video I'll give you..."), provide it right away, or weave it into the video like GrowVeg

does.

3) Make sure you understand how to add descriptive text, keywords, tags and all the SEO components (like closed captioning) on YouTube. Your discoverability through search on YouTube is key to having the traffic you need to build your goal.

Step 3: Send to Email Capture Landing Page or ...

Step 3 has some optional ideas you can try, just like we had optional things for the email capture system. The easiest thing to do is just to send people from YouTube to a traditional landing page with an email capture form. Depending on your business, there could be another video on this landing page, as the people of YouTube are used to that - or it could just be text with bullet points. I'm sure you know exactly what I'm talking about.

But there are other things you could do here. For example, your lead-gen link might possibly lead to an eCommerce site like Shopify. If you use an email capture system like OptinMonster, you can set up code on your Shopify account that will allow for pop ups for email capture. And you can put tracking code on Shopify to build a custom audience for that all-important retargeting ad set up.

YouTube itself has a newly designed vibrant Community interface. It's very easy now to interact with the viewers of your videos. If you love doing Live video, the YouTube version has a super live chat function. You can have conversations with people and they can ask you questions right there. And once they've qualified you to be a wonderful person :-) you can provide links to email capture page or provide them links to products for purchase.

You can see the many options in this step that don't have to be the traditional ways of doing things. As in all new systems - test test test - and check the tracking code.

Step 4: Automation + Personal Experiences

You can have the automation setup move a lead along a discovery channel to qualify your leads by offering them different products, filling out a survey, responding to a poll, joining your social communities - any number of things. This is a pretty basic way of going about business.

The one thing I'd like for you to consider adding here is something that's a little more personal. Remember, people on YouTube are used to watching uploaded videos. Consider adding a regular live video to your regular schedule for YouTube. You can announce this through your email system and your social channels, and start answering those really important questions interactively.

Remember that whatever you're answering needs to be high-quality content, plus that lead-gen offer, or another lead-gen offer, or whatever is the next step in your funnel.

Step 5: Get Personal

This next section might shock you. We have become so used to doing everything automated online that it's a surprising event when someone interacts with us in real-time with a personal email or phone call. My Social Media Manager School business partner Andrea Vahl and I call every single new Premium member of our Group. It has made a huge impact on our reputation as on-line instructors.

Depending on your business, that personal phone call might be before they decide to purchase your product. Even if you end up just leaving lots and lots of phone messages - that's okay. The willingness to talk personally with someone at this point in our marketing evolution is still a strangely exciting thing to people.

There you go - 5 Steps to a Solid Lead Using YouTube. Go make an impact in the world - #Domoregood and crush it on YouTube.

About Phyllis Khare

Phyllis Khare is a two-times Dummies Author – co-authoring *Facebook Marketing All-In-One for Dummies* 1st and 2nd Editions with Andrea Vahl and Amy Porterfield, and she's the author of *Social Media Marketing ELearning Kit for Dummies*.

Phyllis and her business partner Andrea Vahl, have created an online learning center called *Social Media Manager School*, which trains people to be excellent social media managers and consultants. And they recently opened *Social Media Strategy School* to train businesses to develop successful social media marketing strategies.

She's developed a highly acclaimed time-management program for entrepreneurs called *TimeBliss.ME* and she's the social media strategist for *Peaceful Media* — consulting with thought-leader brands all over the world – in many different industries.

Back in the day, Phyllis Khare was a state and national award-winning performer, musician, and educator known as "Miss Phyllis." As a touring singer/songwriter for the Iowa Arts Council for over 15 years, she received numerous grants and awards for her work. She had the amazing ability to keep 600 kids under the age of 10 mesmerized as she taught them through the power of song, dance, and music.

Her children's music has been on sale for over 30 years, and for the last 20 years online for the kids of the first kids who enjoyed it.

She now resides in a fiber-connected farmhouse in rural Iowa consulting and developing online training programs.

Introduction to Conversion

Having someone take action on your website is a challenging task. Whether you are asking them to give you information, buy something, or just watch a video, people often lose interest and move on to the next thing on the internet.

In this chapter, Brian Massey shows you how to take the steps to gather data and test different things to get more of the conversions you need to grow your business. Brian is known as the Conversion Scientist and distills his knowledge of numbers into some easy-to-follow tips.

Conversion Optimization for Busy Managers

Brian Massey

I've learned how to DO many things in my careers as a computer programmer, technical salesman, corporate marketer, and two-time entrepreneur.

However...

The most truly valuable things I've learned are not how to do things, but how to get things done. As managers of people, this is the skillset that ultimately makes us successful as managers and business owners.

So, rather than teach you how to do conversion optimization on your website, I'm going to show you how to manage the creation of a website, advertising campaign, email campaign, social media campaign, or any digital online effort designed to get strangers and prospects to become customers and evangelists for what your business offers.

This is what conversion means.

By the time you're finished with this chapter, everyone on your team is going to think you've become a conversion expert. You will not be, nor should you be. Instead, you will know the right questions to ask, and be able to evaluate the answers you're given.

For some on your team, this is going to be very annoying.

This is because it will result in a series of shifts in culture for your team. This is the only way. The first cultural shift is completely in your control. It involves you getting over yourself. I did it over the course of my career as a conversion optimist. In test after test, I learned that my amazing powers of intuition were not really appreciated by website visitors. Not at all.

The good news is that I learned to use data to be more intuitive and insightful, and I can do the same for you. We are going to make data your personal genius, on call at any time.

Shifting Cultures

Once you have made the shift, the next shifts in culture will involve helping your digital marketing team get over themselves. This is done primarily by modeling the behavior yourself.

For example, if your designer asks your opinion of several mockups of a new ad or page design, you should throw your arms up in the air and exclaim, "I'm not a f***ing designer! Show me some data!"

There are two times in the design process in which cussing is appropriate: when you're trying to implement cultural change, and after the launch of another unsuccessful digital campaign or website. My goal is to shift the cussing from the latter to the former.

Here's another example: When your copywriter sends you the copy for a page, declare, "I'm not a writer! Send me a printout." Don't open it in word and rewrite it. Remember, you're over yourself. Just because you own a copy of Word doesn't mean you can write. Fix the errors and then ask her how she's going to validate that the copy is going to perform.

If you are early in the cultural realignment process, you may get blank stares from the professionals. This is temporary. Soon your primary job will be to ask hard questions about your business and your marketing and your sales. Their job will be to collect some data to answer those questions.

As a manager or business owner, only you know the important questions to ask.

This is the heart of what we call conversion optimization: collecting data to help you make good decisions about the online portion of your business. This data is available to your team cheaply, quickly and early in the process. As a manager, you should be nervous about relying on the opinions of you and your team when you can easily put your work in front of dozens, hundreds, or thousands of others.

Today, it is much more expensive to test a web page or campaign by launching it than to collect some good data to support the design decisions.

The people running your ad networks – your PPC Adwords and Facebook ad accounts – already get this. They use behavioral data to decide what offers to run, what keywords to target, where to advertise and how much to bid on clicks. Conversion optimization is the application of data to the development of websites, landing pages, shopping carts and lead forms.

As a manager, you have the ability to call bullsh*t on bad data. If your designer tells you that he read your marketing study from last year to support his decisions, is that enough?

Here are some rules of data to help guide you in your evaluations:

1) Big **sample sizes** are better than small sample sizes.
   How many people have reviewed the copywriting? How many people responded to the survey? How many visitors saw the landing page test? How many converted?
   When we are shopping for a product, we don't pick the five-start product with only six reviews. The sample size is too small.

2) **Quantitative** data predicts the future better than qualitative data.
   Qualitative data captures the emotions, motivations and preferences of people. Quantitative data captures the kind of data that can be used in statistical analysis.

Examples of Qualitative and Quantitative data:

Qualitative	Quantitative
Open-answer survey questions	Survey questions that have a scale from 1 to 5
Recordings of people using your website	Heatmaps of visitors interacting with your web pages
Focus groups	Taste tests

3) **Behaviors** are better than opinions.
   This is where the term "behavioral" science comes from. If we can measure visitors as they solve a problem for which your business offers a solution, we will get more honest answers than if we ask them why the act the way they do. Humans lie when asked to explain themselves. It's not that we are inherently dishonest. Our brains are designed to rationalize our decisions, especially when we don't know why we made a decision.

4) **Prospects and customers** are more reliable than strangers pretending to be prospects and customers.
   Sometimes it makes sense to employ the input of people who may not be like our true prospects. We can do this to collect a larger sample size of data. But these stand-ins are not as likely to behave like a potential customer. Stand-ins work better for consumer goods with broad appeal than for products appealing to targeted markets.

5) The more **recent** the data, the better.
   Fresh data, right out of the oven is usually best, all other things being equal.

6) Data **over time** is better than data collected at one point in time.
   Data collected over weeks, months or years contains variations caused by seasonal changes and natural market changes. For example, people make different decisions on weekdays than they do on weekends. Business people behave different at month's end than at the beginning of the month.

Apply the Rules to Make Good Decisions.

Let's put some our rules of good data to the test.

Your copywriter created some new copy for a landing page. Your marketing manager reviewed it and you'll also review it.

Sample size? Three (3) people. That's low.

Are the three of you applying **quantitative** analysis? Well, it's just your opinions, so it's very qualitative.

Are your opinions **behavioral**? Nope. Just what you think is good.

Are you three **prospects or customer**? I don't care how long you've been doing this, you are not and you don't understand what they're going through. You're too close to the problem.

The review of this copy is **recent**. You have that.

However, your review comes at one point in time, not **over time**. Would you judge the copy differently on the weekend?

This is why we generally do a terrible job of creating copy and designs in our team.

How could we get some improved data to help us shape this copy into something truly persuasive? In other words, how could we optimized the copy for conversion before we launch the landing page?

We could increase the sample size. Ask the designer to do a mockup of the page with the copywriter's work. Take it over to UsabilityHub.com and show it to 25, 50 or 100 people on their site. Each will answer several questions about the page, delivering some more qualitative input. And you have increased the sample size.

These participants are more like your prospects than you are. Like your prospects, they are being introduced to your company for the first time.

Based on the input from this study, you may come up with several different headlines. These can be tested by creating different mockups and doing a "preference test" at UsabilityHub. Here 25, 50 or 100 participants will tell you which headline they understood best based on questions you ask. This is a more quantitative approach. One or two headlines should rise above the others.

These tests only cost about $2.50 per person and can be completed in a day. Author's Note: I don't have any stock in Usability-Hub, but I wish I did.

UsabilityHub is just one of the services that are springing up to serve marketers and managers, providing ready access to people who can help us make good decisions.

The designer may come in with two or three page designs. After exclaiming that you're not a f***ing designer, take the mock-ups over to Tobii and have 10 or 25 people read the page while tracking their eyes. This can now be done with regular webcams for a few hundred dollars per study. You'll see where the design is working and where it is failing.

Scoring Data

Each kind of study produces data with varying degrees of quality.

Data Source	Sample Size	Qualitative?	Quantitative?	Prospects and Customers?	Recent	Over Time?
PPC Adwords Data	✔	✔	✔	✔	✔	✔
Customer Survey		✔		✔	✔	
Focus Group					✔	
Email Click-through Rates	✔	✔	✔	✔	✔	
Preference Test		✔			✔	
Website Analytics	✔	✔	✔	✔	✔	✔
Live Chat Transcripts				✔	✔	✔
AB Split Test	✔	✔	✔	✔	✔	✔
On-site Feedback	✔			✔	✔	✔
Eye-tracking Study	✔	✔	✔		✔	
Live Session Recordings			✔	✔	✔	✔

Each kind of data will answer different questions about the design of your campaign. The shift in culture of your team will be the desire to find a way to collect some data to support their decisions.

The Best Data Come After Launch

Ultimately, you are going to launch the thing. When you do, the data you collected during development will give you confidence that you are launching high-performing creative.

This is the time to collect some of the best data: large sample size, quantitative behavioral data on your prospects and customers. These are some tools you should have running underneath your website to collect this amazing data:

1) Real-time Analytics like Google Analytics or Adobe Analytics
2) Mouse Tracking and Scroll Tracking Heatmaps
3) Session Recordings

Once you've launched, you can begin collecting what we call the "Supreme Court" of behavioral data: AB tests, or split tests. This method of data collection answers very specific questions about your website and pages with data that meets all of the rules. This data are more difficult to collect and it is easy to misinterpret the data.

Wade on In. The Data's Fine.

By the time this has gone to print, the landscape of data-generating services will have expanded. It will be cheaper and easier to collect this data. Nonetheless, here are some of the tools we use at Conversion Sciences to answer burning questions for our clients:

Question: What headline and images deliver immediate understanding of what a page is about?
Data sources: 5-second test, preference test, question test

Question: What questions are we not answering for our web visitors?

Data sources: Live chat transcripts, on-site surveys, thank you page surveys

Question: Does the layout of my ecommerce product pages make it easy to buy?

Data sources: Heatmap reports, Tobii eye-tracking study

Question: What are my visitors' primary care abouts?

Data sources: Ecommerce ratings and reviews, customer survey, on-site feedback

Question: Should I use long-form copy or short text on a page?

Data sources: AB test, question test

Question: What options should I put in my main navigation

Data sources: Prototype user testing, navigation test, AB test

Question: Which pages on my site are causing new visitors to leave?

Data source: Web analytics

If you are overwhelmed with the plethora of tools, don't worry. As the manager or business owner, you only need empower your team with the expectation that they use these tools to make good decisions. Provide them with a little budget and some training to get familiar with the tools.

And when they come to you with this sweet, business-changing data, you can decide if it's enough to proceed, or ask for more.

There is always more data to be had.

About Brian Massey

Brian Massey is the Founder and Conversion Scientist at Conversion Sciences. He is the author of *Your Customer Creation Equation*. His rare combination of interests, experience and neuroses were developed over almost 20 years as a computer programmer, entrepreneur, corporate marketer, international speaker and writer.

How We've Built a Profitable Business in a Highly Competitive Environment (and How You Can Do It Too!)

Emeric Ernoult

Agorapulse is in the social media management space. If you know that space, you know how competitive it is. If you don't know it, here are a couple of facts to illustrate what I mean by "competitive."

- An exact match search for "social media management tools" in Google leads to 945,000 results.

- Hootsuite, the leader in this space (targeting SMBs), has raised north of $260M. Yes, you read that right. Its challenger, Sprout Social, has raised $60M. Sprinklr, the leader in the enterprise segment, has raised $239M.

- The CPC bid you have to match to on AdWords to be displayed on "social media management tools" search queries is $12. That is $12 per click, not lead.

- When you search for startups providing social media management tools in Crunchbase (the most comprehensive startup database), you end up with 1,025 results. That's 1,025 companies competing in a space that's not even 8 years old.

We launched Agorapulse in this space and we're doing well, against all odds, and despite most investors' opinions that we would never make it in such a highly competitive space.

How did we make it? This is our story.

A competitive market is a good thing.

That's a very important point. I've learned this one the hard way.

In 2001, my co-founder and I started our first startup. It was a revolutionary new concept that didn't exist at the time: online social networking.

I know, we were visionaries ;-)

But there was no market for an online social network in 2001. It failed.

In 2004, we pivoted to a B2B play, trying to sell our technology to large businesses and organizations wanting to build their own private social network.

Here again, there was little existing interest. It barely survived.

But when you enter a market with hundreds of thousands, or even millions of potential customers, there's a big difference! When we entered this space, we no longer had to:

- educate our market
- convince them they need a product like ours or
- fight on prices because there is a market value for your "thing"

Having fierce competition comes with its challenges, but the hardest of all challenges is *not to find your market.*

It doesn't matter if the competition is fierce.

When I read the following post written by Alex Turnbull *(https://medium.com/@alexmturnbull)* from Groove *(https://medium.com/@GrooveHQ)* I had an epiphany:

Should you choose a competitive market or an untapped one? (https://www.groovehq.com/blog/friday-qa-november-04-2016)

In 2014, we were already operating in this competitive market and I had some serious doubts about where we were in it.

Business was painful. It was taking forever to get profitable. I wrote about our story (and past struggles) here:

Agorapulse 2016 year in review: growing from 100k to 245k in monthly revenue (MRR) as a self funded business *(https://medium.com/agorapulse-stories/agorapulse-2016-year-in-review-growing-from-100k-to-245k-in-monthly-revenue-mrr-as-a-self-funded-cd1174a7eb3)*

It was only when I realized that playing in a huge market was our best chance that I started to relax about our future.

Accepting that growth in such a market will take time was hard at first for me to swallow. You might feel the same way.

But if you take the time to execute well, differentiate yourself, think out of the box, and fill the gaps left by larger competitors, you can only win at the end.

Getting a small chunk of a $1B market is doable if you execute well for long enough. It will lead to a good business, maybe even a great one if you're lucky.

But the same amount of effort and the same quality of execution will only lead to a small business in a $100M market.

In a nutshell, if your market is huge, you can make it.

Look at email marketing, CRM, or invoicing/accounting software: all are very, very competitive spaces with a bazillion of vendors and very, very big (and rich) market leaders. Still, there are way more than one successful business in each category.

Pipedrive *(https://medium.com/@pipedrive)* as succeeded in the highly competitive CRM market led (with a bullet) by Salesforce.

Groove *(https://medium.com/@GrooveHQ)* has flourished in the intense help desk market dominated by Zendesk.

MailChimp *(https://medium.com/@MailChimp)* has become a

superstar in the (more than) highly competitive email marketing market with no VC funding at all!

These companies share the same three things in common:

- They didn't play "by the book" of their market.
- They focused on differentiating themselves to stand out.
- They identified a gap in the competition and filled that gap

Let's dig in to these three crucial factors.

When you have bigger / richer competitors, you can't play by their book.

If you enter a market where large and already successful competitors operate, don't copycat what they're doing.

If you do, you'll immediately be outclassed. You can't afford their AdWords campaigns. You don't have the funds for Silicon Valley executive salaries, and you can't shell out the cash for their fancy offices.

So don't try to beat them at their own game. Change the game.

Our competitors buy AdWords keywords at $10 a click and they've built $200k websites with more landing pages than one can count. They've created offerings for everyone, from Mom and Pop businesses to Fortune 500 companies.

If we had tried to do all of that, our business would be dead by now.

But here are the things you CAN do in a competitive market:

- Design an **innovative UI/UX approach for your product**.
  The competition is most likely relying on a product interface that's several years old. THEREIN LIES YOUR OPPORTUNITY, as it did for Pipedrive, Slack and AdEspresso *(https://adespresso. com/)*.

- **Focus on what makes you unique as people**. Larger companies are way too big be seen as human beings anymore. You can. Rand Fishkin does a great job at that with Moz. You can definitely relate to him as much as to his company. So does Alex Turnbull *(https://medium.com/@alexmturnbull)* from Groove *(https://medium.com/@GrooveHQ)*. They both do it a little differently but the underlying principle is the same: the founder(s) behind the business create helpful content, readers/users appreciate, they become interested in the business behind the people.

- **Build an "unconventional" team**. These larger players will probably hire local employees in their "big city" office. They will hire college graduates and people who have past experience in their job. They will be expensive. Very expensive. And they'll have hundreds of them. As a new challenger in a market, you can choose a different path. Hire remotely (https://medium.com/agorapulse-stories/building-a-remote-business-should-you-go-all-in-or-should-you-keep-an-office-f03705eee523) so you can tap into markets that have less expensive cost of living. Hire people with great potential but no experience on the job (and train them). By taking an unconventional path, you can easily have a great team for more than half the cost of doing it the "conventional" way. It will come with challenges, for sure, but if you do it right, you'll do more for less, guaranteed.

Smaller player = more agile.

We've grown from a team of 12 to a team of 37 in 12 months. 37 is still very small, but still, I can already feel the difference in our execution speed. It's not slower, but it's definitely not 3 times faster.

Growing a team introduces a lot of friction. Especially in a remote, worldwide work environment. And all large companies operate in a remote environment as they always have several offices / floors!

Expanding a worldwide team also usually implies operating in several languages, maybe even dozens of them. That adds friction.

It means going upmarket, down market, and expanding your reach to other niches. That adds friction.

In a nutshell, as your company grows, you inevitably become slower relative to your headcount.

That said, if you focus on the right market segment and the

right part of your product, you'll execute faster than the big boys and girls.

Focus on battles you can win today.

If you have a smaller team with fewer resources, you simply can't fight head-to-head with your larger competitors on *all* fronts.

But you can win *specific* battles by focusing your agility on getting one thing better than them.

Pick a niche, pick a feature, pick a marketing channel, anything they are not great at and can have an impact on and do that better than they do.

Then rinse and repeat.

Doing this will eventually lead you to compete head-to-head and win the war. But for now, just win that war one battle at a time.

Use your competitors' brand awareness to your advantage.

Larger competitors have probably been around for longer than you do. They definitely have a much larger marketing budget. Their SEO is stronger. They get a ton of organic referrals without lifting a finger.

That's the magic of brand awareness. It's great when you have it. It's tough when you don't and your competitors have it.

It doesn't matter that your product is better. The one that people know is the one that gets all the toys. Awareness is everything.

So what can you do? While there's no magic formula, let me share what we've done in that area.

First, identify your 2 or 3 "best" competitors. Those are the ones you keep being compared to when you're talking to prospects. For us, it overwhelmingly was Hootsuite and Sprout Social.

There is a TON of other social media tools out there but these two kept popping up. (And they still do.)

These competitors need to have enormous brand awareness. Check out the organic mentions our two big competitors get on the Web compared to us. We're in blue.

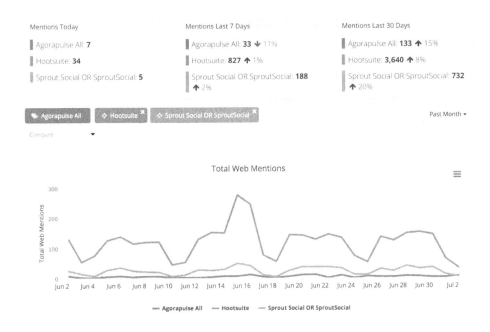

Monitoring of mentions of Agorapulse vs. Hootsuite and Sprout Social using Buzzsumo *(http://www.buzzsumo.com/)*.

Once you've picked the 2–3 competitors, identify what makes you stand out against them. Maybe it's a set of specific features you have and they don't, a market segment you're serving better than they do, or a pricing gap you're filling and they don't.

Create assets that benchmark you against them based on these differences and use them to your advantage. If these assets come from third parties, it's even better!

In our case, we've leveraged 3 different advantages:

1—Our tool gets better user satisfactions than our competition.

Our guts knew it, our early users told us so, but frankly, it was very hard to let the world know: our software was more users friendly than the leader in our space.

What we did very early on was to invest a LOT of time in getting our users to review us on the major review sites. The one that worked best for us was G2Crowd *(https://www.g2crowd.com/)*. I basically reached out personally to all our users, as the founder and CEO and offered (free) advice. At the end of the call, I kindly asked if they would give us a review.

In the course of 5 years, we eventually got more than 360 reviews. But look how good we look on G2Crowd compared to Hootsuite (that has 1,022 reviews!):

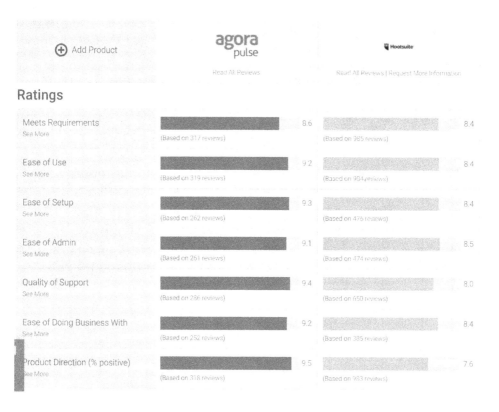

I'd call that a home run. Best on every topic.

So now, it's not our guts telling us we're better, it's hundreds and hundreds of real user reviews, most of which come from Hootsuite users themselves!

Once you have an asset like that, you can create marketing materials that leverage these results and/or get bloggers to create them on their own.

Pretty darn powerful if you ask me.

2 — Our pricing is much better for teams.

In their path to more profit, our two biggest competitors have continually increased their pricing. It's pretty common to go up-market as you grow.

It's usually not a bad thing to do. We did the same by killing our lowest plans as they got us the highest churning users. The more a user pays, the more likely they'll stick with your product.

But when you increase your pricing, you will create gaps that are not necessarily made of "bad fits" but who will suddenly find your product way too pricey.

That's what has happened to businesses managing social media profiles with a team. As Sprout Social and Hootsuite basically have a "per user" pricing model, every time they increase the cost per user by $20, they're actually adding a lot of cash to a team of 5 or 10!

We saw the opportunity here: a LOT of small and medium teams would soon find their plans unbearable. So we've engineered our pricing to be more team friendly.

Check out the results with price comparison tool build by Seriously Social (https://social-media-management-pricing.iag.me). It's mindblowing how expensive our competitors can become with 10 team members and 20 social profiles:

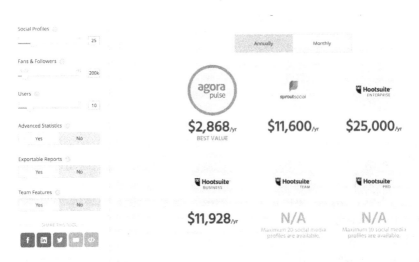

That move alone got us a lot of success with teams. They are also the ones that stick with us the longest.

Good bet.

3—We have a useful feature that the "big" guys don't offer.

Once you have the assets highlighting your unique advantages, use them in your marketing over and over. Retarget your traffic with them and reach out to bloggers mentioning your competitors to bring your solution (and its differences) to their attention.

If you leverage these assets consistently, they eventually help raise your awareness by showing your market that you exist. Again, like winning the war, this needs to be done one step at a time.

The bigger the competitors, the more opportunities are out there. Seize them.

As businesses become larger, they change course. They may start with a simple set of features but as they become bigger and more successful, they will add more and more features, leaving room for a smaller competitor to become better than them at one specific feature.

For example, as Zendesk was getting bigger and bigger, its product became fairly complicated to onboard and learn. Groove and Help Scout seized that opportunity and built help desks that were really simple and efficient for the needs most small businesses have. They created two very healthy businesses by leveraging the gap left by Zendesk as it was getting more and more complex to fulfill the needs of larger businesses.

Another area where gaps are created all the time is pricing.

Be careful: competing on "we're the cheapest for anything you need!" is never a good idea. But having a pricing that's better suited for a specific set of customers can be a great idea.

As I mentioned earlier, as Hootsuite and Sprout Social kept increasing their pricing on a "per user" basis, they became extremely expensive for teams.

We saw an opportunity here and decided to not price our tool per seat in 2015. Later on, we'd reintroduce a cost per seat but still included several team members in each plan, making our pricing structure a no brainer for large teams.

But we're not cheaper for everyone. Hootsuite, for example, has a free plan for solo businesses that we can't—and don't want to—compete with.

Pricing is always a big decision factor and if you look carefully at your competitors' pricing and listen to your market, you can always find gaps to fill.

The road to happiness is in your goal setting.

That will be my final take, but it's a biggie.

If you operate in a market that's already crowded and where the competition is big, strong and rich, having the goal to "dominate" that market eventually is probably the best way to set yourself for depression—not to mention financial ruin and a bunch of disgruntled employees.

But if your goal is to capture a good niche in that market, or a big enough market share to have a profitable sustainable business, then you stand a good chance and you may find the path to profit and happiness.

Our largest competitor has more than 450,000 paid users and our second largest has close to 17,000. If my goal was to get more than them without their already solid brand awareness and their millions of VC funding, I'd probably stress myself to death for the next 10 years.

That's not the life I want.

I have the more reasonable short term goal to get to 5,000 paid users, giving us around $600,000 of monthly revenue. Nothing "huge" or unicorn-like, but a very, very profitable and healthy business that will make our 40 people team very well paid and beyond happy.

Once we'll get there, we'll raise the bar, probably to $1M MRR, and so on. I don't have a big bold goal that I'm not sure I can achieve. I set my goals one step at a time.

Don't chase impossible dreams, especially in very competitive markets. Chase a dream that you can reasonably achieve and grow from there. Who knows, you may become a unicorn, but don't make that a goal. Is it really a good goal after all?

Remember what happened to the unicorn frappuccino *(https://www.washingtonpost.com/news/food/wp/2017/04/20/please-dont-get-it-starbucks-barista-flips-out-over-unicorn-frappuccino/)*?

About Emeric Ernoult

Emeric is the Founder and CEO at Agorapulse. He started his first social media software in 2000 when social media was not even a thing yet. He runs his 40 people remote team from Paris and has grown his company to be one of the key player in the social media management space without any external funding. He loves to help fellow entrepreneurs, ask him anything on Twitter at *eernoult*, he'll get back to you!

Introduction to Leadership

Part of being a business owner is leading your company. Whether your company is 100 people or just you, as the owner, you need to make the right decisions and lead the company to more profits.

In this chapter, Erik Qualman shares 10 leadership lessons he has learned from Steve Jobs. Erik is a world-renown speaker and the author of best-selling books *Socialnomics* and *Digital Leader*.

10 Lessons I Learned from Steve Jobs

Erik Qualman

How unfortunate it is that visionary Steve Jobs is no longer walking among us or breathing and inspiring the next steps towards a technological era. This misfortune truly reminds all of us the value of life. As a tribute, I have included ten leadership lessons I learned from Steve Jobs:

1. Simplify

Jobs required a simple iPod without any buttons or even an on and off switch. This seemed implausible for the engineers working on the project, but Jobs would not bend. The engineers were pushed to their limits as the iconic scroll wheel emerged from the efforts. Jobs indicated, "That's been one of my mantras — focus and simplicity. Simple can be harder than complex: You have to work hard to get your thinking clean to make it simple. But it's worth it in the end because once you get there, you can move mountains."

2. The power of "NO"

Jobs is just as proud of the numerous products he killed over the years as the ones that were monumental successes. At one point, he worked hard on a device similar to the Palm Pilot, but appropriately killed it to focus on the cell phone market. The iPod and iPhone resulted from this decision. Today, my company creates a monthly "Not For Now" project list.

3. Money is overvalued

"Being the richest man in the cemetery doesn't matter to me... Going to bed at night saying we've done something wonderful... that's what matters to me." Innovation has nothing to do with how many R&D dollars you have. When Apple came up with the Mac, IBM was spending at least 100 times more on R&D. It's not about money. It's about the team your work with, how you're led and how much you can grasp.

4. It's not what you say; it's how you say it

Jobs keynotes and launches products to spellbound audiences. Not all products under Jobs were the most cutting edge on the market; however, consumers perceived them to be. Part of this reason was Jobs overzealous demand of secrecy around products. This secrecy helped feed consumer desire for the product once it was revealed. That is the critical point –perception becomes reality. Part of Jobs success was based on the notion that, "Your customers dream of a happier and better life. Don't move products. Instead, enrich lives."

5. Borrow good ideas and make them great

Jobs and Apple did not create the computer mouse, podcasting, or the touch screen, but they recognized their value and integrated these innovations into their products. Sometimes it is not about inventing the "thing", it is about inventing a way to make the "thing" better.

6. Shun the Majority

Jobs' actions epitomized the mantra of, "if the majority were always right than we'd all be rich". Like Henry Ford before him who said, "If I asked the public what they wanted they would say a faster horse." Jobs typically abstained from focus groups and gave the public what he thought they needed. This worked the majority of the time, but when it didn't it became a chance for him to fail forward into the next project, taking the lessons with him. "Here's to the crazy ones, the misfits, the rebels, the troublemakers, the round pegs in the square holes... because the ones who are crazy enough to think that they can change the world, are the ones who do."

7. Eat Your Own Lunch

There is a saying in Silicon Valley that you need to eat your own lunch before someone else does. Jobs had the conviction to do this with the introduction of the iPhone, knowing it would, and did, cannibalize the sales of the flagship iPod. Letting go of the familiar and embracing the unknown is a real test of leadership.

8. Strive for perfection

The night before the opening of the first Apple store, Jobs didn't like the look of the tiles so he had them all ripped and replaced. Right before the iPod launch, Jobs also had all the headphone jacks replaced so they were more "clicky".

9. Small Teams

Jobs didn't want his iPhone team to be muddled with pre-conceived notions around the mobile market so he had the team placed in a separate building. While this rubbed some employees the wrong way for not being selected, the results are irrefutable. The original Macintosh team had 100 members. Whenever the team reached 101 members, they would have to reshuffle and remove someone from the team. Jobs' belief was that he could only remember 100 names. [Source: Leaner Kahney, The 10 Commandments of Steve," Newsweek, page 35, September, 2011]

10. Follow Your Heart

"If today were the last day of my life, would I want to do what I am about to do today?" And whenever the answer is "No" for too many days in a row, I know I need to change something."

It's sad to think that Jobs passed at the young age of 56. Yet, his legacy lives on in the lessons he's instilled in others – like me. My hope is you find these lessons as helpful as I have and begin to incorporate them into your life. For further reading on the habits of digital leaders, please see my book *Digital Leader*.

About Erik Qualman

#1 Best-selling Author and Motivational Speaker Erik Qualman has performed in 49 countries and reached 25 million people this decade. Qualman was voted the 2nd Most Likeable Author in the World behind Harry Potter's J.K. Rowling. For availability: 617-620-3843 or eq@equalman.com

His work has been used by the National Guard to Nordstrom to NASA.

His animation studio Equalman Studios has produced work for Disney, Raytheon, Chase, Verisign, Hearts on Fire, and many other brands.

Introduction to Live Video

Live video is gaining more traction as a go-to medium to get noticed, get more reach, and brand yourself as an expert. Facebook currently gives live video more preference in the news feed and YouTube just released their own form of Live video.

In this chapter, Jamie Turner shares his best tips on how you can get started with live video and grow your business. Jamie is the founder of 60 Second Marketer and a frequent guest expert on CNN.

Insider Secrets on Getting The Most from Live Video

Jamie Turner

Is video a big deal right now? Just ask Forrester Research – they say that videos are 50 times more likely to get a first page ranking than traditional text pages. In another study, Cisco found that video will account for about 69% of total user web traffic in the coming year.

So, yes, video is a big deal. Which means that you need to be taking a deep dive into how to use it to grow your sales and revenues.

In this chapter, we'll explore tips and strategies you can use to integrate video marketing into your own business. Ready to dive in? Let's get started.

1. Understand the Distinction Between Live Video and Pre-Recorded Video

There are two different kinds of video we'll be talking about in this chapter – live video (as in Facebook Live, Instagram Live, Live Streaming on YouTube, etc.) and pre-recorded video (which upload a pre-recorded video to most major social media platforms including Facebook, LinkedIn, YouTube, etc.).

Live video is often shot unscripted, typically with a smartphone or a laptop. Pre-recorded video usually has a little more pre-production going on with lighting, better sound, and possibly even a teleprompter.

2. Rehearse Your Intro and Your Outro

There's nothing worse than a live video (or a pre-recorded video) with a weak opening and closing. Before you shoot your video, rehearse your intro and outro so that it rolls off your tongue easily. Rehearse it multiple times because when the camera is on, you'll be inclined to stumble a little bit before you get your legs under you.

3. Plow Ahead Even if You Stumble

We live in an age of authenticity, so if you do stumble (during a live video shoot), don't worry, it just makes you more human. Keep going, and don't draw attention to it. If you're shooting a pre-recorded video, you might enjoy the flexibility of doing a re-shoot if you stumble, but if it's a minor flub, you can always leave it in – people gravitate to other people who are real, authentic, and vulnerable.

4. Start with the End in Mind

Every great marketing campaign starts with a list of goals and objectives. Your goal might be as simple as building awareness for your brand. A more specific goal might be to drive clicks to your website. Or, you could get even more specific by having a goal of driving prospects to a landing page where they fill out a form and become a lead for your business.

No matter what your goal is, it's important to have a specific result in mind. So, first things first – think through what your end game is and write it down so you can keep you sights on the desired outcome.

5. Get Familiar with Your Live Video Platforms

Meerkat and Blab are dead, which is a bummer. Periscope is owned by Twitter, which means as long as there's a Twitter, there'll be a Periscope. That leaves us with Facebook, Instagram, YouTube, Snapchat, and a few others as your primary live video options.

Getting set up on Periscope, Facebook, Instagram and the other live video options is pretty easy. Just check their websites for plenty of up-to-date instructions. All that said, actually creating a video on any of those platforms is another story altogether – the technology is simple, but the nerves can get in the way.

Fear not. We live in a short-attention-span digital world where what you did last week (or in the last hour) is quickly forgotten. Plus, people are surprisingly forgiving to people who give live video a try. So don't be afraid – dive in and start using the platforms.

6. Create an Engaging Title

The title of your video may have just as much of an impact on your traffic as the actual content itself. As a starting point, a great title has the ability to instantly grab the attention of a potential consumer. Additionally, using appropriate keywords in your title increases the likelihood that your content will show up on search engines. Also, when it comes to SEO, it is important to keep in mind that Google owns YouTube, so there is a strong connection between SEO and video.

7. Become a Storyteller

Effective video content tells a story to the consumer as opposed to strictly "selling" to the consumer. Furthermore, it is important for businesses to recognize the power of emotion and to use it to their advantage when creating video content. The Digital Marketing Institute notes that businesses should use this tactic in an effort to appeal to their customer's needs and desires.

8. Keep it Short and Sweet

According to a study *(https://www.videobrewery.com/blog/18-video-marketing-statistics/)* conducted by Visible Measures, nearly 1/5 of all viewers will discontinue watching a video within 10 seconds or less. Many people feel that video content should be as short and to the point as possible, but your audience (or your needs) might be different, so be sure to test which length appeals to your audience the most.

9. Remember That Many People will be Watching on a Smartphone

According to YouTube *(https://www.videobrewery.com/blog/18-video-marketing-statistics/)*, consumption of mobile video increases by 100% every year. Most platforms are automatically set up to be viewed on a mobile device, so from a technology standpoint, there's not a lot to worry about. Just try to keep context in mind – that is, that your viewer might be sitting at a bus stop, in a mall, or at a restaurant.

10. Mobile User Engagement

Whereas desktop viewers of video content *(https://www.videobrewery.com/blog/18-video-marketing-statistics/)* are known to only stick with a video for 2 minutes or less, this number increases when it comes to mobile viewers. iPhone users typically watch for 2.4 minutes, while Android users are estimated to engage with a video for 3 minutes. Users who watch video content on iPad's have the longest user engagement of all at around 5 minutes.

11. Make Content Educational in Nature

One of the best ways to use video for your business is to focus on educating your viewers. A majority of viewers search for videos that offer informative content such as advice, tips, news, etc. This type of content has been found to be more effective than strictly promotional video content.

12. Add Music

Another useful way to take advantage of video content is to incorporate music. Music can strike a variety of emotions in the consumer. Use music that fits the overall mood of the message and provides a more well-rounded experience for users. But remember, the music is supposed to be a bed underneath your video. Keep the volume low – probably even lower than you think. The purpose of music in the kinds of videos we're talking about here is to carry the listener through the video, not to interrupt it.

13. Upload to Your Site First

Be sure to upload your pre-recorded video to your own website first as a way to get the most bang for your SEO buck. And don't forget to tag your videos with keywords that are important to you. Descriptions and tags allow Google to make sense of your video content and give it the ability to properly rank your video.

Additional Tips and Tricks

Here are several additional tips and tricks to keep in mind as you take a dive into video.

1. Get the Right Equipment

If you're a small business or a start-up, you'll probably want to shoot your videos off of your mobile device. That's fine, if you're trying to save a few dollars. That said, it's a good idea to invest in a microphone that plugs into your smartphone. You can purchase a good lavaliere microphone for less than $100, which will improve the sound quality significantly. (Side note: Be sure to spend an extra $30 on an extension cord so that you can shoot video with your microphone from more than 10 feet away.)

2. Shoot Using the Right Lens

Did you know that the selfie lens on your smartphone isn't as high quality as the lens on the opposite side of the selfie camera? If you're going to shoot from your smartphone, be sure to shoot using the lens on the back side of the phone – as in, the lens on the opposite side of your selfie lens. That's a higher quality lens and will improve the quality of your videos significantly.

3. Invest in Video Editing Software (or Outsource Your Editing)

If you're shooting live video for Facebook, Instagram, or any other platform, then you won't really need video editing software. But if you're shooting pre-recorded video, you might want to invest in software that improves or enhances the quality of your footage. If you're on a Mac, then Movie will do the trick for basic videos. If you're on a PC, then it might be worth investing in Camtasia, Adobe Premiere, or some other video editing software. Also, don't forget that you can also hire a third party to edit and sweeten your video. You'd be surprised at how cost-effective that can be.

4. Think Big and Create a Campaign

While stand-alone videos can be effective, think outside the box when it comes to video content marketing. Creating a theme or campaign of content-rich videos allows you to reach greater exposure. A campaign also allows consumers to easily access more information on the same topic, which provides your business the ability to build upon your brand identity.

5. Don't Forget a Call to Action

A call to action is important for businesses to build a following for their brand. Businesses can ask consumers to visit a specific website, subscribe to their channel, sign up for their newsletters, or any number of other requests. Don't miss out on the opportunity to ask users to continue to engage with your brand by implementing the above techniques.

6. Provide a Link and Embed your Content

Be sure to provide a link to your viewers to drive traffic to your website. Additionally, make sure to embed your video on your own website. By implementing these tactics, you will provide multiple opportunities for your business to increase traffic and grow an audience. Google's algorithm takes in to consideration how many times a video is viewed. So, essentially, by embedding your video into your website or other platforms, the views you receive gets added to the total views on YouTube.

According to Forbes *(https://www.forbes.com/sites/forbesagencycouncil/2017/02/03/video-marketing-the-future-of-content-marketing/#5886930a6b53)*, it is estimated that video content will account for more than 80% of all web traffic by 2019, making it all the more important to implement each of the tactics outlined in this chapter. Good luck! And keep us posted on your results.

About Jamie Turner

Jamie Turner is an internationally-recognized author, speaker and TV news contributor who has helped The Coca-Cola Company, AT&T, CNN and other global brands tackle complex marketing problems. He is the CEO of SIXTY *(https://sixty.company/)*, a marketing consultancy and advisory firm that has worked with The Coca-Cola Company, Holiday Inn, SAP and others. He is also the CEO of 60SecondMarketer.com, a business blog that is read by hundreds of thousands of people around the globe.

Jamie is a regular guest on CNN and HLN *(https://60secondmarketer.com/blog/2016/09/23/will-brad-angelina-divorce-impact-brands/)* on the topics of business, digital media and leadership. He is the co-author of *Go Mobile*, which was the #1 best-selling mobile marketing book on Amazon when it was first released, and *How to Make Money with Social Media*, which is now in its second edition.

Introduction to Better SEO

Search Engine Optimization (SEO) is the name of the game in this online world. You can have the best content on the web but if no one can find it, it doesn't matter. There are many best practices to getting your content found but they can be overwhelming to keep up with.

In this chapter, John Jantsch shares his proven technique to get his content found using a tool called BuzzSumo. John is the author of *Duct Tape Marketing* and founder of the Duct Tape Marketing Consultant Network and his blog regularly ranks on the first page of results in Google.

How to Use Buzzsumo to Hack Your SEO

John Jantsch

Take your pick - would you rather have better content or better SEO results?

As you might have guessed - it's a trick question.

When it comes to content and SEO, you can't have one without the other. But, I hear the moaning - the constant need to produce content ideas makes feeding the content beast one of the bumpiest elements of the digital marketing world.

One of the tools I use to make this easier is a tool called Buzz-Sumo. It helps me ensure I'm on the right track with my content strategy in an effort to improve my search engine results.

BuzzSumo helps guide me when I'm trying to stay on track with my editorial and SEO strategy by suggesting content that has proven to engage readers. I've written about BuzzSumo in other posts *(https://www.ducttapemarketing.com/buzzsumo/),* but today I really want to take a deep dive into how to use this platform to hack your SEO and be a better and more efficient content marketer.

Essentially, BuzzSumo is a search engine that tells you how many shares a piece of content has received in places like Facebook, Twitter, and LinkedIn. It also tells you who shared the content and who linked to the content, so it's a great little research tool for all things related to content.

Let's put it this way, if BuzzSumo were a band, I would buy front-row tickets to their concert. Yes, I'm that big of a fan. In essence, the platform is a search engine that ranks content based on how often an article is shared.

Content research

Often, when people think about research in regards to SEO, keyword research comes to mind, but another type comes to mind for me as well: content research.

BuzzSumo is a great tool for doing content research which can be very useful for determining specific forms of content that you may want to produce. If a piece of content has been shared a lot, you may want to consider developing something similar for your own content (don't copy it, but see how you can improve upon the content and make it your own.)

Think in terms of creating something even more epic than the most shared content around your research topic. So if 10 ways to do XXX is highly shared, come up with 25 ways to do XXX even better.

When it comes to keywords to search for in BuzzSumo, you need to think outside the box a bit and think of terms that may be related to your industry, not the industry itself. For example, instead of typing in "marketing," try typing "SEO tips" and see what new keywords and ideas may show up in the BuzzSumo results (as shown below.) If you are a plumber, you might consider something like "leaky faucet". I'd recommend doing a bit of keyword research before using BuzzSumo so that you have a good list to test out ahead of time.

What you're looking for in these search results are themes, whether they be with keywords, domains, content types, or even influencers that show up repeatedly.

You'll have the ability to review backlinks from the searches and with that, you can develop a list of sites that you may want to target for you or your client to get backlinks from (an increase in authentic backlinks will help to increase your site's SEO), or, you can develop a list of influencers to target knowing what type of content they like to share.

As you can see, doing content research through BuzzSumo can quickly help you generate content ideas to help with your content marketing and SEO efforts which can be far more time consuming and stressful using other means.

Competitive research

You may be wondering what competitive research has to do with SEO. Well, a lot. The whole point of SEO is to outrank your competition in search engine results pages, so it's important to keep tabs on what they are doing. BuzzSumo makes it easy to do that.

Instead of typing in a keyword phrase into BuzzSumo's search box, you can type in a competitor's URL and see what's been the most shared content for them and who is linking and sharing their content. These can provide very valuable data points for your strategy moving forward.

Think about it, you can see the most shared content from any website. You can track your competitors and look for ways to take advantage of their research or you can simply find other industry sites to get ideas on why they might be popular.

Finding guest content

Getting published on other sites is a great way to increase your number of backlinks and boost your SEO. This tool actually has the capability for you to filter "guest content" to see who runs and allows guest content to be posted on their site within the industry.

Make a list and start pitching your great content ideas to other sites that have already demonstrated they like posting guest content. Of course, you're not bound by content you find on Buzz-Sumo, you this is a great approach for local strategic partners as well.

Of course, there's the flip side of this equation - you can also Buzz to find and build a list of people you want to guest post on your own site.

Content analysis

BuzzSumo also allows you learn more about how your content is shared and the best approaches for future content.

With this feature, BuzzSumo looks through all of the articles it shares based on your keyword by network, content type, date published, content length, and related topics (among other filters.) This tied in with the search results can really get you going in the right direction.

For example, when I look through my past content I see that my posts that are over 1,000 words seem to get shared far more than shorter posts.

This is invaluable information to optimize your content marketing and SEO efforts. The more "popular" your posts are online, the more likely you'll be to increase your search rank, so having this data and information available to you to help put your best foot forward in the SEO world is a huge win in itself.

BuzzSumo is a great tool to help round out your editorial calendar and boost your SEO through content marketing efforts.

For more details about how I use BuzzSumo for content marketing, check out this video *(https://www.youtube.com/watch?v=-DOT-6MNd1BY)*. I also encourage you to check out the tool at *buzzsumo.com*.

About John Jantsch

John Jantsch is a marketing consultant, speaker and author of *Duct Tape Marketing*, *Duct Tape Selling*, *The Commitment Engine* and *The Referral Engine* and the founder of the Duct Tape Marketing Consultant Network.

His latest book, *SEO for Growth - The Ultimate Guide for Marketers, Web Designers, and Entrepreneurs*, is changing the way the world thinks about SEO.

Introduction to Virtual Reality

Virtual Reality is the wave of the future but how can you use it to grow your business? There are opportunities available now for business owners to use Virtual Reality but also things to think about for the future that the smart business won't ignore.

In this chapter, Martin Shervington shows us what is coming and how we can participate as a business. Martin is an author and a speaker and currently making a BBC Documentary about VR.

Virtual Reality for Content Marketers (AKA, The Rest of Us)

Martin Shervington

"Virtual Reality (VR), to some extent, is a misnomer. The name suggests that there is something unreal about it. It is "virtual" and therefore of value as a novelty perhaps, only tangential to our reality. In truth VR is a representation of the real world, enhanced by the additional possibilities provided by the new medium. As such it is an expansion of our current capabilities, a canvas that's yet to be adequately filled as we are not yet sure what we want to see on it. As technological development accelerates there is only one thing that's certain for the future, the constrained reality of the past, the one that was determined by our locality and the narrow bandwidth of our corporeal presence, will be the one that will increasingly feel unreal and anything digital, including Virtual Reality, will feel deep and vibrant, meaningful in a way that only something highly intentional can be."

David Amerland - *author, speaker.*

Introduction

We've all seen the predictions of the explosive growth[1] for Virtual Reality (VR) flow in our social streams, but adoption by 'the rest of us' non-gaming enthusiasts has not been as expected[2].

In this chapter, I want to give you a perspective on how things may develop for you as a content marketer, without having a fifty thousand dollar budget for one piece of content.

Now: 360 videos

360 videos, which can double up to give a VR experience, have had a big push in the past 12 months with an increase in well priced cameras and Facebook's enthusiastic adoption. So will the world we enter next be a 360 one for you and I as content marketers, or 'something else'? I think a little of both, but mainly something else.

When it comes to 360 video it is the high-end production value that wins out every time in VR. Putting it crudely, crappy 360 video is a waste of time. I've tested mid-range cameras[3] and for 360 they are fine, but not when you look around in VR. As such, and to create that higher end experience, you'll have to shell out a minimum of a couple of thousand but more likely it needs to be $40,000+[4] if you want to compete for attention at a higher level for video content.

The next challenge as a content creator is the nature of narrative you will create in that format. A view of a sunset is great for 10 seconds, but before long attention shifts and people *need movement* as they crave being taken on a journey, and the desire for a storyline begins. If you don't have film making skills, you may well find you invest in the gear and still have no idea. But as VR entrepreneur and storyteller Sarah Hill says[5] it is getting easier but

1 *https://www2.deloitte.com/global/en/pages/technology-media-and-telecommunications/articles/tmt-pred16-media-virtual-reality-billion-dollar-niche.html*

2 *https://www.ft.com/content/f7e231ee-fc84-11e6-96f8-3700c5664d30*

3 *https://www.linkedin.com/pulse/should-you-buy-theta-allie-cam-martin-shervington*

4 *https://www.jauntvr.com/technology/* and *https://ozo.nokia.com/vr/*

5 *https://medium.com/@sarahstories/forced-perspective-how-liquid-cinema-will-change-*

there is going to be a steep learning curve if you are just starting out.

You can use 360s to market, and can add adverts into/onto them; there will be product placement through to straight attention grabbing ads of a variety of types - that is, unless 'drop frame' technology arrives, and is then banned (think 'subliminal messaging' in the cinemas with Tyler Durden[6] at the helm) - but there is a better way - *to look at you being you at a different level*. And that 'you' relates to brands too.

I think it may surprise you where it takes us...

The Future: We Become Artists, Performers, Educators

With Virtual Reality there will be two types of people: consumers and producers. In about three years' time, I would predict the former will be more than 99.9% of people enjoying the ride, and the remaining people will find their voice and build a community around their niche content.

You can do this in several ways:

1) Create your own app, with your own content (costly).
2) Use a White Labeled solution which will act as a Virtual Shelf for 360 photos, plus an audio narrative - I encouraged the good people of Weavr.Space (a project I was on for 4 months) to add in the voice over functionality - perfect as an addition to virtual tours, especially for real estate.
3) Use a White Labeled solution for e.g. 360, and 2D video content[7] - having launched a content platform (3courselunch.com) in 1999 I am seeing the same cycle come round time and time again.
    Putting it simply, people need a home for their content, and a place for the community to find it.

---

vr-storytelling-17e0b61a25f5

6 There as a scene in the movie Fight Club with shows Durden 'splice' movies with content of an adult nature.

7 I believe this will lead to 'content shelves' (like YouTube), and whole new approaches to marketing funnels.

4) Generate content using the apps and share back on Social Media. We can see already that apps like Google's Tilt Brush is allowing VR artists to perform and big brands like Nvidia are paying attention[8].
But what if you are not 'arty in that way'? What if you are a blogger, or a writer? What if you are a process driven YouTube content marketer? Well, I would suggest you look to…

5) Social VR - if you are value learning and teaching, then the answer is to transcend any VR app that may be used as a tool. Instead you want to hone your art, and be ready to perform in a new space.

Social VR

This view has come from nine months of exploration: I see Social VR as the perfect place to deliver content that can 'live forever' - think like video, but in VR, and it can be done 'now'.

We are still early days on the technology being able to deliver what it will in a few years, but here is what we've tested already:

1) People create presentations using a mix of audio and video clips, photos and text.
2) They beam them into a Social VR platform.
3) A community of people attend 'live', and/or.
4) The VR experience is recorded and can be 'replayed' as if it is live when watched.

This technology already exists through AltspaceVR, now owned by Microsoft, allowing for a 'time travelling experience' where you can even re-visit one of your own events and attend in the future. There was a scene in the TV show 'Fringe' which gives you some idea of how this looks and feels, without trying it in VR for yourself. May 2017 myself and Elisa get married in VR, in part for the fun of it but also as it's proven to be a case study of how to run a global event using this technology. You have to write the script (which is the best way to approach it) with 'now' and 'then' both

---

8 NVIDIA powers Tilt Brush Art Contest on HTC Vive *https://www.youtube.com/watch?v=ayH_pwSTlk4&feature=youtu.be*

in mind at the same time i.e. for the live version and the future attendees who won't know any difference to, what will be then, past attendees. It is said that interactable objects can be passed across timelines[9]. If you want to bend your mind then that certainly will.

All in all, this means you can deliver content once, and people experience whenever they happen to arrive.

In the future we can tell our stories, and have virtual visitors from the future watch them as long as the power is still on.

You navigate around the scene, not as a passive observer from a fixed perspective (as is the case on 360 video now), but free to roam.

Think about this for a second: you can deliver a live event once, and give people the link so they can attend *as if it was live*, but in the future.

VR recordings as a concept is a leap in content marketers' ability to efficiently build brand, community and (if they know how) to create conversions to e.g. opt-ins.

I've tested all of this. It works. I've heard from the community manager at AltspaceVR (the app I used to put on VR comedy shows) we have almost 1700 people register for the last 'Meta-Geekonomics event (a comedy game show, using hundreds of video samples.) In another event I achieved a 50%+ conversion rate from a call to action to give email. When you can let the event run once a day, or on demand, you have a content marketer's dream - effective use of new technology to drive a quantifiable marketing results.

The key is this though: content, within a VR context.

Good, relatable content that drives people's emotional responses within this new world.

My content has taken me 500 hours+ to create - with themes of VR and Artificial Intelligence running through it. All in all, I like the idea of us being artists with a sense of humor. And Meta-Geekonomics even has a mission 'To make Ai chuckle the moment it wakes up and becomes self-aware', which myself and Elisa find amusing.

---

9 Introducing VR capture *(https://www.youtube.com/watch?v=Z27kl9a877U)* - this shows passing objects to a future self

As it stands, right now you can get attention around 'unique VR' experiences - and also build your brand in the mainstream as a 'breakthrough' persona. Myself and my betrothed, for instance, will be in a three part BBC documentary on Cardiff Bay (where I've been living.)

Beyond the future: Artificial Intelligence (Ai)

How Ai and VR will work together is down to imagination, until it happens. But one of the most obvious applications will be connecting social data (from existing sources) and feeding back into changes of the content that is delivered. If you think social media is personalized now, simply add in social data (preferences, connections) plus real-time eye tracking (and later 'telepathy' will enter the equation[10]) and you are on the way to unique worlds of experience being created.

Next Action Steps for content marketing:

You'll need the following to get started in VR as a content marketer:

1) The best equipment for the job - right now that means spending upwards of $2000, but by mid-2018 most new VR headsets will come powered by Leap Motion, so you will even be able to see your hands using a mobile setup[11].
2) Just like when we all had to learn to be 'good on camera', you will need to polish your communication skills and work on 'your voice' to connect well with virtual avatars.
3) A 'funnel mentality' - I've been testing a process of using 20 minute 'Keys' that move people through a 'Gate' - which is basically the process Internet Marketing has been using for years, but applied to VR.

---

10 *https://www.theguardian.com/technology/2016/jun/14/zuckerberg-telepathy-face-book-live-video-seinfeld*

11 *https://www.qualcomm.com/news/releases/2017/02/23/future-vr-here-qualcomm-and-leap-motion-work-together-demonstrate-natural*

4) The communities in VR right now are not what you are used to - so unless you 'bring your community with you', you will need to learn a new approach to engaging with them, and most of all to hold their attention with what you deliver.

Finally...

I wrote an article review on Israel and Scoble's book *The Fourth Transformation* for Weavr.Space when I helped them launch start 2017, and how I ended it was like this - there was a quote from a Facebook post by Robert Scoble that I'll finish on, which is:

"In the future, we are most likely to become artists, and I think that that is the piece that gives me the most hope. More than the technology, more than the applications, is that somehow it brings out the best of us, and art is something to be shared." Let's be artists, and play much more. With the robots (well, Ai) taking our jobs I think it may well mean I finally get my comedy act moving too."

Which is exactly what I have done, and I hope you connect with the play outside of tech that is sitting there, just waiting for you to discover.

About Martin Shervington

Martin Shervington is business consultant and online community builder with a postgrad degree in Organizational Psychology.

He has 17 years' experience of consulting on marketing, stats and conversions and how to influence people's behaviors online. He has been doing stand-up comedy about VR for 3 years, and been researching how VR can be used by marketers (without huge budgets) for 12 months.

Introduction to LinkedIn Branding

LinkedIn is one of the premier social sites for businesses to network, but so many business owners aren't optimizing their profile. First impressions are everything. When you have a profile that stands out, you win business.

In this chapter, Viveka Von Rosen shows us all the ways we can make our profiles better and all the ways to encourage new connections, leads and sales with LinkedIn. Viveka is one of the world's foremost experts on LinkedIn, speaking all over the world and having written many books on LinkedIn.

36 Ways to Rock Your Personal Brand on LinkedIn

Viveka von Rosen

Tom Peters first wrote about Personal Branding way back in 1997. In an article called *The Brand Called You,* he said "Regardless of age, regardless of position, regardless of the business we happen to be in, all of us need to understand the importance of branding. We are the CEOs of our own company: Me Inc. To be in business today, our most important job is to be head marketer for the brand called You."

If you want to control how you are seen by the world, then you really need to stand out. And one of the best places to create and share your brand is on LinkedIn. Why? Because there are 500 million users - many of which could help you build your business. But if you don't have a strong brand on LinkedIn, you could be invisible to those prospects, or worse yet, lose credibility. And that will cost you business!

Creating a strong personal brand on LinkedIn starts with having a strong personal profile. Which means having a strong visual presence and engaging "client-centric" copy. Make sure your background images, media and logos reflect your website and other digital platforms. And when writing (or repurposing) the copy for your profile's Summary, Experience and Projects section, make sure that you focus on your audience's wants and needs. Most people make a list of their services on LinkedIn – focusing on the features of their company and not the benefits to their prospects. If you have one, your LinkedIn Company page should also reflect this strong visual and audience focused content.

Getting Started

Get Focused

Can you help anyone with a face? Anyone online? Then you won't help anyone at all!

It would seem that the more people you could help in and with your business (whatever that business is – teaching, training, engineering, mothering, job-seeking, nonprofit, volunteering, eating bonbons) then the more successful you would be. But that is not the case. The more focused you can be on who you are, what you do and who you serve the better!

Be Clear

Clarity is key to personal branding. The clearer you are about who you are, what you do and who you serve, the better you will relay your skillset and the more likely you are to "convert" your "prospect" into customer or client.

Your Elevator Speech

Who Are You?

Can you answer that question in a sentence or less? In marketing, we call it an elevator speech. What is your elevator speech? Specifically, who are you? What makes you different from everyone else out there? What makes you different from the other person who does what you do, where you do it and with the same clients? Knowing that is the first key to successful branding.

What Do You Do?

It seems obvious, but the second question you must answer is, "What do you do?" And depending on the country you live in, who you are is in fact NOT what you do. Sometimes answering what you do is easier than answering who you are...but both are important to your personal brand.

Who Do You Serve?

Another important question is: "Who do you serve?" Being very clear on the people, companies and industries you serve will help you to create the look and feel of your personal brand. If your client base is 50ish professional men, then a light pink and frilly logo with lots of touchy feely language might not be the way to go. My first business (personal and business coaching) was focused on women. It was named AlwaysExtraordinary.com. My website was pink and orange. Now I work (mostly) with corporate sales teams and business owners, tilted slightly to the male variety. My website is black, orange and blue.

Visual Branding

To tell the truth, I'm a little graphically challenged. In fact, I think one of the reasons I focused on LinkedIn was because until 2009, it really didn't have many visual features. But LinkedIn had to go change all that (and I had to hire a graphic artist). Let's look at the many different ways you can visually build your brand on LinkedIn!

Get Ahead by Getting a "Header"!

LinkedIn now allows you to upload a background image on your personal profile. This is one of the easiest (if you are graphically inclined or can pay for it) ways to emphasize your personal brand on LinkedIn. If you have or work for a company, then you can incorporate (with permission) their branding... colors, fonts, logos etc., into your header or background image.

The latest background image template is 1584 x 396 (yes, I don't know why they couldn't just go with 1600 x 400. That would be much easier to remember.) Just remember to leave room for your head! (I mean your picture on LinkedIn.)

What to Do If You Don't Own Your Own Company

If you don't own your own business, and the company you work for won't let you incorporate their branding, or you are looking for a job, you can still use the header image to reflect who you are, what you do and whom you serve. See why those initial questions were so important?

Jiving With Your Audience

If you work with (or want to attract) a bunch of Millennials, then create an image that jives with them. (And don't use the word "jive.") If you work with old ladies like me, then use images we will find attractive (I can't resist a Kate Spade hand bag.) But don't use half-naked ladies... I know many men like them, but that is simply not appropriate for LinkedIn. Which is, after all, still a business-networking site!

Upload Your Picture

Upload your image. Really. And make sure it resembles you in this century. Don't use a logo. Not only because we are talking about personal – not corporate – branding. But also because it goes against LinkedIn's user agreement. Section 8.1 of LinkedIn's User agreement states that you cannot: "Use an image that is not your likeness or a head-shot photo for your profile; Create a false identity on LinkedIn;... Misrepresent your identity, including but not limited to the use of a pseudonym."

When uploading your image, make sure it looks enough like you so that when you go to a conference or a trade show or a job interview you won't get blank stares due to a complete lack of recognition. I remember a blind date once; walked right by the guy who was 100 pounds and at least 15 years older and much more follicley-challenged than his picture. I should have kept walking. Just saying....

Upload Media

You can also upload all sorts of media now! You can link You-Tube and Video links and upload PPTs, Word docs, PDFs and gifs. If you have media that helps to support your personal brand, then make sure to get it on LinkedIn!

Find Some Long Lost (Media) Gold

Do an audit of your computer files and folders to see what you have that you can upload to support your personal brand. Do you have examples of your work that you can share? (Just don't spill the beans to a secret recipe!)

Google Knows All

Google yourself. There might be something online that you can share a link to that will help to support your personal branding of expert, genius, guru, maven... Oh wait, that's me. But anyway, take a look and see what you find. Obviously just business or brand related. And you should be wearing clothes in all media.

Add Your Company Logo to Your Personal Profile

One more visual to add (which you might have seen, but didn't know how to do it) is to "tie" your company logo in with tying your logo and company page together. To do this you may have to: add or simply edit your existing Experience section, choose your company from the dropdown menu to connect it to your company page, (which has the added benefit of creating a navigation link AND embedding your logo on their personal profiles.)

Branded Copy

Naming Yourself

A rose by any other name.... is something else. Please take minute to make sure you have your name on LinkedIn. Make sure you spell it correctly. Unless you are ee cummings, please take a minute and capitalize your name!

Only your Name

Have your name and ONLY your name on LinkedIn. You might see some folks have their area of expertise, (it's your brand, right?) in the last name field: Viveka von Rosen: LinkedIn Expert. That goes against LinkedIn's User agreement;

"Do not add content that is not intended for, or inaccurate for, a designated field (e.g. submitting a telephone number in the "title" or any other field, or including telephone numbers, email addresses, street addresses or any personally identifiable information) for which there is not a field provided by LinkedIn".

If LinkedIn catches you doing it they will make your profile un-findable in the search. How do I know? Cause I did it and they did it.

Your Professional Headline

Nothing says Personal Brand like "Title at Company". Just kidding. You should really take a minute or two to think about how to customize your Professional Headline (that section right under your name) on LinkedIn. You have 120 characters to describe who you are, what you do and whom you serve. (Is that beginning to sound familiar?)

Do it in Word First

When you are writing content for LinkedIn... any content... from your name to your Summary Section, then PLEASE create it first in a Word document. It will help you to:

- Catch REALLY silly spelling errors "Cheif Marketing Officer"
- Find grammatical errors
- Add special characters
- Count your characters

And it's a backup in case LinkedIn deletes your account for having something other than you last name in the last name field!

The Crucial Summary Section

Another forgotten but crucial section on LinkedIn is your Summary Section. (Sometimes known as a Background section.) You have 2000 characters to describe in detail who you are, what you do and who you serve. That last part, who you serve, is very important here.

WIIFT

You might have heard a very popular phrase in the 90's: "But what's in it for me?" or WIIFM? But Social Sales, Social Marketing and Social Branding are all about the WIIFT... what's in it for them? If you can speak their language, and assuage their fears and fill their needs, you'll find yourself... and your brand... to be more successful in LinkedIn.

Are You Experienced?

Your Experience Section can be more about you and what you do. You have 2000 characters to describe your company and what your company does. You can list services, features and USPs (unique selling propositions) here. Again, what makes you and your company different from everyone else?

Education

Whether you have your MBA from Harvard or a degree in the "Hard Knocks of Life," consider adding your education to LinkedIn. It is part of who you are. You have 2000 characters to describe what you did in school and why it's relevant to who you are today. For instance, I got my Masters in Native American Women's Autobiography. Ok.. not really. Well, kind of. Anyway, that might not SEEM like the natural progression in education for a Social Media Guru such as myself, but in fact the ability to empathically engage with a culture has made me pretty good at marketing or sales. See how you can spin that?

Skills

Skills. List them. That is all.

Ok, for those of you I have not convinced, while you will get endorsed for skills you don't have by people you don't know, it's still good to list your skills. If you know who you are and what you do and whom you serve, you'll have a pretty good idea of what (up to 50) skills you can add to LinkedIn. And if you don't add them, LinkedIn will!

Endorsements

Endorsements are more of a Facebook "like" than a true testimonial to your awesomeness. But they still count. Make sure to list your Skills (mentioned in the previous chapter) and then go ahead and endorse a few of your friends. Also, make sure you have the endorsement feature turned on. Duh. Here's an article I wrote all about how to get more endorsements *(https://www.linkedin.com/pulse/linkedin-endorsements-do-you-need-more-just-ask-viveka-von-rosen)* on LinkedIn.

Adding Projects

For those of you who are contract laborers or consultants... there are Projects. (The rest of you can use them too.) Projects are great because they allow you to share details about the work you do without listing each and every one of the hundreds of jobs you've done for the past 10 years. That might make you look like you can't hold a job for folks who don't bother to read the part that says "consultant" or "contractor". Part of building your personal brand is proving you have deep experience in a particular industry or skill set. But you don't want to look like you have employment ADD either.

Publications

Now I get that not everyone out there is a Published Author. But a lot of you are content creators. If you write a blog or a newsletter or have an eBook or use LinkedIn Publisher or guest post or have a journal, you are now considered a Publisher on LinkedIn. While you probably don't want to list every blog post you ever created, I do recommend you do choose a few that really support your brand and add them to Publications. Do an audit of your files and Google... you might have forgotten about a Publication relevant to your Brand.

Organizations

You might want leave Political and Religious Organizations out of LinkedIn, (unless that IS your brand) but I strongly suggest you add the organizations and volunteer work that you do. Both lend an emotional quality to your brand... that can help to increase positive brand sentiment.

Proving Your Brand

It's all well and good to tell people how awesome you and your brand are, but it's even better when other talk about how great you are! Here are some ways to encourage positive brand sentiment with endorsements, testimonials and recommendations!

Asking for a Recommendation

LinkedIn has a feature that allows you to ask for and give recommendations. Unless you already have them, it's kind of hard to find. The easiest way to ask for a recommendation is to go to *www.linkedin.com/rec/ask*. You can also find them at the bottom of your profile (if you already have them) by clicking on "manage".

Hit Up Your Friends

You can only get recommendations from people you are connected to (what would be your friends if we were on Facebook right now.) So if you are not connected to someone you want to get a rec from, then go and invite them to connect now.

Asking: Best Practices

Don't go with LinkedIn's default copy when asking for a rec-ommendation. In the Subject field remind them how they know you; "Could I ask you for a recommendation for the work I did with you (at this place) and when."

In the body of the recommendation you might give them some bullet points - so that have something to grab ahold of:

"Can you please write me a recommendation for the work I did with you in the Caymans at the marketing conference last November? I'd love it if you could write about my knowledge of my topic, reliability and reliability... and of course my fantastic singing voice."

If you know the person is really busy and you know them pretty well, you might even write your own recommendation for them to customize and use.

Testimonials

If you have a testimonial that is stellar, but the author is not on LinkedIn (or won't connect to you), then you can always upload the testimonial as an image, as a PDF, or even put a bunch of testimonials together in a SlideShare presentation. You can even copy and paste shorter testimonials right into the "description" sections of your Summary, Experience, Education and even Projects sections.

If a picture is worth a thousand words, what would a video testimonial be worth? No excuses! I bet everyone reading this book has a video feature on his or her cell phone, or knows someone who has a cell phone. Get some video testimonials, upload them to YouTube or Vimeo and get them on LinkedIn.

Personal Branding through Company Pages

So that is your Personal Profile, but what about Company Pages?

According to LinkedIn, over 80% of their 500+ million members want to connect with companies on the platform. Do you have a company page? And are you making the most of it?

Description

You probably already have a company description on your website. So by all means copy and paste that text into the word document you use to create your new company profile description. And add those keywords! You get up to 2000 characters to describe your company. As we did in the summary section, make sure to use white space, special characters, bullets and capitalization

Try customizing your description specifically for LinkedIn. Is your Company profile description speaking to your LinkedIn Audience? You might even address them directly saying something like: "We are glad you found our LinkedIn Company profile. Check out our Services and Products page for special offers! As a special offer to our followers we will be sending Company updates with promotions and discounts as well, so follow our Company! We are here to..." (and then give them a list of benefits.)

Background Image

Most companies understand the value of visuals, but get lazy when it comes to LinkedIn. I see many cut-and-paste patch jobs from website banners or other social banners. Companies miss a real opportunity to create visually arresting images that grab their viewers' attention (and hopefully get them to scroll down to the updates.) With a world of content at your fingertips, it's worth taking a little extra time to have multiple, great options.

Branding Across All Your Employees' Profiles

Growth starts at home. Make sure that your employees have connected their profiles to your Company Page. Start with getting your employees to add or edit their existing "experience" section, choosing your company from the dropdown menu to connect it to your Company Page. This has the added benefit of creating a navigation link and embedding your logo on their personal profiles. Also, encourage them to share Company Updates through their networks.

Updates

LinkedIn members will be able to see your company status updates both on your Companies overview page, as well as on their own homepages, as long as they are following you.

Sponsored Updates

Finally, consider sponsoring an ad to drive traffic. While this can seem daunting, it's a great way to create relationships with new audience members.

Market Your Company Page

Companies forget that they need to market their LinkedIn pages just like any other product. That means investing time and money. At the very least, make sure that your mailing list knows you have a Company Page. Give them a quick link they can easily follow, and put your Company Page link in your email signature with your LinkedIn personal profile URL. It makes all the difference.

You can give them a reason to follow your page by focusing on what's in it for them. No one wants more noise on their timeline, but if you have a special promo code or unique insights that they can't get anywhere else – they might "Follow" you for that.

Wrapping Up Your Personal Branding with LinkedIn

There you have it! Over 8 pages of actionable tips you can use TODAY to create a stronger brand on LinkedIn! Want over 101 ways to Rock your Personal Brand? Feel free to purchase my book: LinkedIn: 101 Ways to Rock Your Personal Brand. Or if you need help creating a better branded profile on LinkedIn, then go to *www.vengreso.com/personal-branding-package-comparison*

Having a stronger profile will increase your visibility, help you to attract more relevant prospects and make you more money!

About Viveka von Rosen

Viveka von Rosen founded one of the first LinkedIn training companies, Linked into Business *(http://linkedintobusiness.com/*)* in 2006 and in 2017 cofounded Vengreso *(vengreso.com)*, the largest full spectrum digital social selling provider in the world.

Known internationally as the "LinkedIn Expert", she is author of the best-selling *LinkedIn Marketing: An Hour a Day and LinkedIn: 101 Ways to Rock Your Personal Brand!*

As a contributing "expert" to LinkedIn's official Sales and Marketing blogs and their "Sophisticated Marketer's" Guides, she is often called on to contribute to publications like *Fast Company, Forbes, Money, Entrepreneur, The Social Media Examiner*, etc.

Viveka takes the LinkedIn experience she has perfected over the past 10+ years and transforms it into engaging and informational training (having provided over 100K+ people) with the tools and strategies they need to succeed on LinkedIn.

Introduction to Content Marketing

Content marketing helps businesses get found. These days having a blog with fresh content isn't an option – it's a must. But if you aren't writing the content people want to read, your site won't grow. More traffic to your site leads to more business growth.

In this chapter, Michael Brenner shares with us his go-to research tools so that you can create the right content. Michael is a speaker and author and well-known expert on leadership.

6 Content Marketing Research Tools You'll Fall in Love with

Michael Brenner

If you want to know how to create content that people are actually searching for, you need to become a content marketing research expert.

But it doesn't have to be that hard or expensive! To uncover the top trends and topics of interest within your industry, you just have to roll up your sleeves and dig a little bit. You might even have some fun in the process.

Read this, and you'll have the power to discover what content is making the search engines tick and the social channels hum, with these powerful – and easy-to-use – content marketing research tools.

Google Auto-Fill

Google *(https://www.google.com)* does a lot of the work for you, revealing what search terms people are using with the search engine's auto-fill feature. You've probably used this tool hundreds, or more realistically, thousands of times, without even realizing just how useful it is for informing your content marketing strategies.

Simply start typing in the beginning of a question or phrase. Omniscient Google will do the rest. The auto-fill function displays the most popular searches, offering you a gold mine of on-trend long-tail keywords – for free.

Play around with auto-fill to really get an idea of what it can do. Want to know the meaning of life? There you go.

So when I want to learn what marketers are looking for to help develop their content marketing strategy *(https://marketingin-*

Q the meaning of life is

G Google Search

the meaning of life is 42

the meaning of life is to find your gift

the meaning of life is to give life meaning

the meaning of life is

the meaning of life is that it stops

the meaning of life is death

sidergroup.com/content-marketing/content-marketing-strategy-lacks-content-strategy/), look no further than the auto-fill box for 'content marketing strategies.' This is what you'll get:

Q content marketing strategy

G Google Search

🕐 content marketing strategy

content marketing strategy template

content marketing strategy example

content marketing strategy 2017

content marketing strategy pdf

content marketing strategy definition

Search for **content marketing strategy** with:

With this information, you know marketers are after examples *(https://marketinginsidergroup.com/content-marketing/best-content-marketing-examples/)*, templates *(https://marketinginsidergroup.com/content-marketing/tips-tools-and-templates-to-build-your-content-marketing-strategy/)*, and the latest content marketing strategy tips *(https://marketinginsidergroup.com/content-marketing/content-marketing-tips/)* for 2017.

Click on 'content marketing strategy template' and scroll to the bottom of the search engine results page to get more related search terms. Now you can get even more specific and spot-on

Searches related to content marketing strategy template

content **plan** template **excel**	content marketing strategy **checklist**
content **plan** template **for social media**	content marketing **plan pdf**
content strategy template **pdf**	content marketing **proposal** template
content marketing strategy **framework**	content **plan example**

for your audience by creating content that offers a 'content plan template for social media' or a 'content marketing strategy check-list.'

This is exactly what searchers are after. You are now equipped to provide the solution. See, you don't have to be psychic to excel at content marketing.

Google Trends

Google has even more to offer in terms of free research to help you craft the content your audience wants to stumble upon. Google Trends *(https://trends.google.com/trends/)* is your go-to source for finding out what are the most important topics right now in relation to your search terms. You have access to a magnificent amount of search data with this research tool.

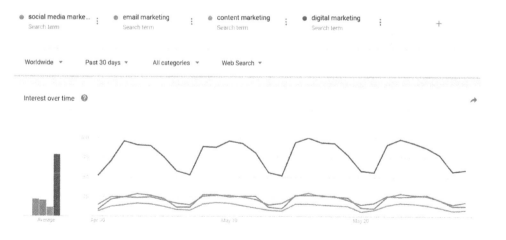

Google Trends will show you related queries, interest by region, as well as a comparison of related search terms – over different time durations ranging from since 2004 to the past hour.

Not sure what direction to go in for a particular topic? Is your marketing team having an in-house discussion on what's a more relevant keyword topic – social media marketing, email marketing, content marketing, or digital marketing?

Google Trends will resolve your issue with neat, easy-to-digest data. And, this tool will give you the top 25 related search queries to make your content development even more efficient.

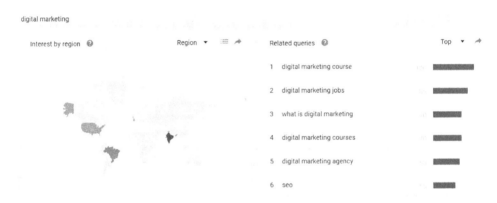

With all this free help, could it be that Google wants content marketers to only create highly relevant, value-driven, useful material? That's correct. Google's vision statement *(http://panmore. com/google-vision-statement-mission-statement)* is, "to provide access to the world's information in one click." The search engine has offered these free, powerful research tools so you can do a better job. Use them!

BuzzSumo

I LOVE this tool. BuzzSumo *(http://buzzsumo.com/)* allows you to create your entire content marketing strategy with one tool. It's comprehensive, intuitive, and it simplifies your research. How to uncover keyword gems and start developing ingenious strategies? Here's a glimpse of how the BuzzSumo process works.

	FACEBOOK ENGAGEMENTS	LINKEDIN SHARES	TWITTER SHARES	PINTEREST SHARES	GOOGLE+ SHARES	NUMBER OF LINKS	TOTAL SHARES ⌄
5 massive **SEO** and **content** shifts you need to master right now ☐ Save / searchengineland.com - More from domain / By Jim Yu - May 17, 2017	437	439	1.1K	9	92	-	2.1K
Tackling Tag Sprawl: Crawl Budget, Duplicate **Content**, and User-Generated **Content** ☐ Save / moz.com - More from domain / By Russ Jones - May 24, 2017	187	157	876	13	71	-	1.3K
Stop overloading your Local **SEO content!** ☐ Save / searchengineland.com - More from domain / By Greg Gifford - May 22, 2017	260	161	799	3	72	-	1.3K
Why Design Still Trumps **Content** in **Marketing** ☐ Save / searchenginejournal.com - More from domain / By Searchenginejournal® - May 25, 2017	458	266	388	51	64	-	1.2K

1) Type in your category or search query. BuzzSumo will generate a list of the most shared articles on that particular search term. You can filter the results by duration, content type, and more – or even check to see only in-depth articles on your chosen topic. You can then review articles to reverse engineer the most popular topics for your audience.

2) With this tool you can also see what the most popular publications are in your industry. Now you can create a list of the best publications to target for advertising or to pitch your articles.

3) Type in the website of a competitor or a top industry publisher. BuzzSumo will show you the most shared articles on the site.

4) You can even look across the social platforms to see which are the most popular in your niche, and the most likely to engage your target audience.

5) Give your content marketing strategy an upgrade with a lit-

tle influencer marketing. When you purchase access to the tool, you can see influencers in your topic area and then reach out to them for guest posts and other influencer marketing strategies.

6) Monitor your content marketing – you can even compare the progress of your content marketing campaigns against that of your competitors.

You can try out this research tool with a free trial, but to get all BuzzSumo's elegant search data, you'll have to sign up for a subscription. The Pro level service is $79 a month, which is a good starting point for small marketing teams and professional bloggers.

AnswerThePublic

AnswerThePublic *(https://answerthepublic.com/)* is a free tool that can make a huge impact on your content marketing research. Sure, the bearded guy on the home page can be a little disconcerting. However, if you think of him as the wise old man of the web, ready and waiting to serve as your own personal content marketing oracle, you'll be on to just how game changing this resource truly is.

Like the other content research tools listed, this one is as simple to use as it is profound in its offerings. Type in your category or keyword and marvel at the results. Plug in 'content marketing,' for example, and you'll get your visual diagram of the 77 relevant questions searchers are using to learn more about the query. Why, how, what, which, when, and where.

From how to do it to why it matters, AnswerThePublic gives you the questions so you can give your audience the answers.

Ahrefs

For the content strategist who likes to take their SEO very seriously, Ahrefs Content Explorer *(https://ahrefs.com/)* is a data-rich resource that will inject an expansive perspective into your keyword and content planning. You can do a lot with this tool:

1) Look up the organic search traffic and backlink profile of any website, including industry leaders and competitors.
2) Get a clear overview of the most popular content for a topic based on backlinks, organic traffic and social shares, as well as an in-depth list of keyword ideas.
3) Uncover backlink opportunities.
4) Use the SERP Checker to analyze search results and accurately estimate traffic potential.

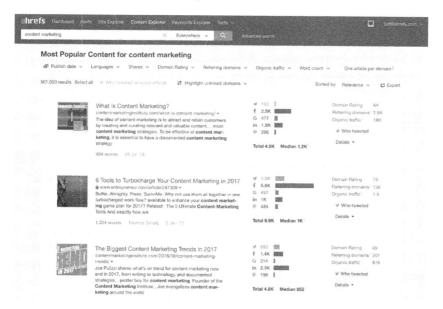

This is one of the most dynamic content research tools out there. It's even recommended by SEO and content experts like KissMetrics Founder, Neil Patel and SEObook's Aaron Wall. Like BuzzSumo, Ahrefs does come with a price. Subscriptions start at $99 per month.

SEMrush

Want to see what keywords your competitors are using to drive organic traffic? Wouldn't it be helpful if you could see clearly how you stand up to other sites in your niche when it comes to search rankings – and track these changes over time?

SEMrush offers a unique look at your site's metrics. It is a practical tool for informing both your content marketing and advertising strategies. The biggest perk? The Keyword Magic Tool. This feature gives you access to over 2 million keyword ideas. You can group by topic, analyze, and create targeted lists, helping to make solid content strategies that are well organized.

With all the information at your fingertips, neatly presented with excellent data visuals, you can take your content research capabilities to a whole new level of precision. This is all without having to spend extra time making sense of all the numbers. The tool does it for you. A basic subscription costs $99.95 a month.

Effective Tools Make Your Content Research Worth It

One of the biggest challenges for content marketers is having to consistently come up with compelling content. If you're not honing in on the most relevant topics and providing answers to the questions your audience is asking, you are losing traction to your competitors. Also, you may be wasting those hours you're devoting to crafting quality content. If people aren't searching for your content, what good is it?

On the other hand, by taking the time to research the industry trends and keyword topics that are getting the most searchers in your niche, every blog post, infographic, or video you publish becomes imbued with impact.

Make a commitment to research. Solid research is the foundation of an effective strategy. And, effective content research tools are the backbone of this foundation. Then flesh out your investigative work by staying on top of popular industry blogs and newsletters, reading trade magazines, listening to podcasts, and following the influencers who are moving in your niche.

Whether you prefer the simple brilliance of Google's free resources or the endless possibilities of content planning subscription services, the more you know, the more empowered you are to make every piece of content count.

About Michael Brenner

As a globally-recognized keynote speaker and consultant on leadership, culture, and marketing, I help companies and reach, engage, and convert new customers. And I help entrepreneurs and leaders to achieve the results they want.

I co-authored the best-selling book *The Content Formula*. And I've written more than 1,000 articles for *The Economist*, *The Guardian*, *Forbes*, *Entrepreneur Magazine* and more. In 2017, I was named a Top Business Speaker by *The Huffington Post* and a top CMO Influencer by *Forbes*.

If you're ready to take your company, your marketing and your culture to the next level, send me a message or head over to *https://marketinginsidergroup.com*

Introduction to Connecting

What are you doing to make the most of your social media activity? Are you regularly making time to actually make meaningful connections in real life from the online interaction?

In this chapter, Andrew Davis shares his simple rule for how to grow your business by having more targeted and meaningful conversations. Andrew is an engaging speaker and author and consults with brands all over the world.

The Simple Routine Deigned to Turn Online Interaction Into Offline Action

Andrew Davis

The 4-1-1- Rule

Diving into social media can rapidly become a time suck. Before you know it, you are spending hours every week creating social media graphics to promote blog posts which link to YouTube videos designed to increase email subscribers who share your content on Twitter. All of it can become overwhelming, exhausting and before long, you question the value it adds to your business.

Social media can be a valuable tool in your marketing and sales arsenal if you are clear about exactly why you are using it. So let's clear up a quick misconception.

You are Not Looking For Links or Likes

It is too easy to find yourself pining for more likes, fans, followers and friends. In our quest to increase our "engagement" on social media we focus more and more on the latter and less and less on the former. We become media moguls instead of social savants. The most successful business people I know spend less time looking for likes or sharing links on social media and instead focus on interacting with the audience they serve.

The more time you spend interacting, supporting, and serving your audience the more likely you will find yourself building online interactions that lead to offline action.

Also, you will quickly realize that the most valuable interactions you have on social media are not with your company or your brand, they are with you.

You Are the Brand

Social media is powered by billions of social interactions: millions of Tweets with @replies and #hashtags, Facebook posts, comments, Likes and messages, YouTube annotations and replies, Reddit threads, and even Instagram stories.

Here's the rub: a social interaction is "an interpersonal relationship between two or more people that may range from fleeting to enduring."

See that? It says "two or more people." A social interaction, by definition, cannot occur between an inanimate object, an anthropomorphized brand, or even a personified logo. This means, all those Tweets from your branded tweet stream - they do not matter - they are inauthentic. Those posts are fake and forced attempts at social interaction. They are a prime example of traditional marketers trying to feign authenticity in an environment powered by authentic personal interactions. Here's a hint: people power social media. Not logos.

Brands Are People-Powered

Here's the good news. You do not need a high-priced ad agency or brand consultant to help you develop your brand's voice. In fact, your 'brand voice' is the sum of the individual voices that make up your company's employee roster. It is the voices of the people who power your vendors and of the customers who buy your products. In today's online universe everyone has an audience, and every individual has a voice. You no longer have to inauthentically personify your brand, your team does this for you.

So, instead of chasing likes, links, fans, followers, or friends, let's focus on creating conversations. The kind of conversations that generate real business.

Let's use the 4-1-1 rule.

The 4-1-1 rule

Remember 4-1-1?

If you are old enough, you might have dialed 4-1-1 from a landline for directory assistance. That's right; you used to be able to pick up any telephone, dial 4-1-1, and ask a real, live, operator any question you wanted. It was as if you had a human version of Google at your fingertips. (You still can dial 4-1-1 from most phones, but today it is automated, and it is not near as much fun as it used to be.)

It just so happens that 4-1-1 is an excellent ratio for building your social media routines and maximizing your online relationships. The 4-1-1 rule is designed to help you disseminate information and encourage conversation while you promote the products and services you sell.

Here's the simple ratio:

For every four (4) pieces of relevant, original content you share from others, re-share one (1) piece of content from one of your fans or followers. This social currency earns you the right to share one (1) piece of self-promotional content or insight.

For example: if you're looking to engage with prospects on Twitter you might spend some time finding four pieces of relevant, original content from other influencers or content creators and share them with your followers. The key here isn't to just post the link, but pull out the most interesting insight and contextualize it for the people you are looking to attract. Now, look at your Tweet stream and find one individual who follows you to interact with. Ask them a question, share a piece of their content. Comment on their blog post, or even better - respond to a question they have. Now, you've earned the right to share something that benefits you. Go ahead, share a promotion, ask for a favor, Tweet something you've created.

You don't create an audience on social media. You earn it.

Stop thinking of social media platforms as simply a content distribution and promotion platform. Think of it as a community building tool.

You want to attract an audience - not drive people away. In general, trying too hard to promote yourself does the latter. Feed content snacks to your audience that will establish you as both a participant and a leader in the conversation.

About Andrew Davis

Andrew Davis is a best-selling author and internationally-acclaimed keynote speaker. Before building and selling a thriving digital marketing agency, Andrew produced for NBC's Today Show, worked for The Muppets in New York and wrote for Charles Kuralt. He's appeared in the *New York Times*, *Forbes*, *the Wall Street Journal*, and on NBC and the BBC. Davis has crafted documentary films and award-winning content for tiny start-ups and Fortune 500 brands.

Recognized as one of the industry's "Jaw-Dropping Marketing Speakers," Andrew is a mainstay on global marketing influencer lists. Wherever he goes, Andrew Davis puts his infectious enthusiasm and magnetic speaking style to good use teaching business leaders how to grow their businesses, transform their cities, and leave their legacy. His two books: *Brandscaping: Unleashing the power of Partnerships* and *Town INC: Grow Your Business, Save Your Town, Leave your Legacy* are Amazon.com best-sellers.

Introduction to Fusion Marketing

Are you taking a "holistic" approach to your marketing efforts? How do online and offline marketing work together to grow your business faster?

In this chapter, Lon Safko explains his "Fusion Marketing" approach which will turbo charge your marketing efforts and help you only focus on the things that are working well. Lon is a worldwide speaker and author of *The Fusion Marketing Bible*.

Pulling It All Together
Fusion Marketing

Lon Safko

Fusion Marketing

Overview

As many of you know, I am the author of the best-selling book, *The Social Media Bible*, and my newest best-seller is called *The Fusion Marketing Bible*. Fusion Marketing is about "What's next", it's what comes after social media. Fusion Marketing is actually an entirely new form of marketing.

I discovered Fusion Marketing as a result of constantly being asked in interviews, "So, what comes after social media?" I would think to myself, "Social media has change the way the world markets, sells, and communicates forever. And, it has caused us to change at speeds we have never seen before with technology" and you want to know what's next?

I decided to take that question on as a personal challenge. I asked myself, "Where will marketing and sales organizations be in say, five years? How will we be treating traditional, digital, and social media marketing?" That's when I realized that Traditional Marketing + Digital Marketing* + Social Media Marketing = Fusion Marketing!

I realized that even now, if you are calling yourself a "Social Media Expert", then you're announcing to the world that you have been left behind. If you're an expert in Facebook and Twitter, then you're trying to build an entire marketing strategy restricted to using only one or two tools from all of the marketing tools available today. And, the reason we aren't seeing the ROI from social media is, Facebook is not a strategy. Twitter is not a strategy. LinkedIn is not a strategy. They are only tools. We'll get to what is a strategy later.

If you're still stuck looking at social media as a stand-alone marketing technology, then you've been left behind. Today the term V.P. Social Media Marketing sounds normal, but it is already as obsolete as V.P. of Billboards. The first companies that recognize that social media marketing is only one set of marketing tools out of many, will be ahead of the curve.

Fusion Marketing is the next generation of marketing that brings all of our 6,000 years of traditional "push" or "monolog" marketing, the exciting digital marketing tools* of the Internet, and social media "two-way communication" or "dialogue" marketing and fully integrates them into one seamless toolset that will accomplish every objective you set at no additional cost to you or your company!

*Digital marketing tools are different from social media as they don't imply two-way communication. Social media tools such as Facebook, Twitter, LinkedIn, and others imply a post and a response. Digital tools do not. Examples of digital tools as SEO (Search Engine Optimization), SEM (Search Engine Marketing), RSS (Really Simply Syndication) and eCommerce. These are all necessary for marketing and aid in your being found on the Internet, but doesn't imply two-way communication.

Fusion Marketing is such a totally new concept of "Fusing" all of your marketing tools that it has been accepted by the United States Patent & Trademark Office as "Patent Pending".

As part of the Fusion Marketing concept, I also invented a tool to help you implement your Fusion Marketing Plan called the Safko Wheel. You can get this development tool for free with the purchase of The Fusion Marketing Bible book or you can just make one from scratch.

This article is about how Fusion Marketing and the Safko Wheel works, and how you can use these tools to discover hidden ROI opportunities in your marketing without spending a cent more. Fusion Marketing is a 12 Step process and here's how it works.

(Trust me... It's fun and it really works!)

Fusion Marketing & The Safko Wheel – A 12 Step Process

Set Up

Get the book / Wheel or just make one. Cut out or create the 20 "Traditional Tool" cards and the 20 "Digital / Social Media Tool" cards and at least one Wheel (a 20-pointed starburst). Place the 20 Traditional Tool cards around the Wheel as you see below.

Traditional Tool Analysis

Step 1 – Select Your Traditional Tools

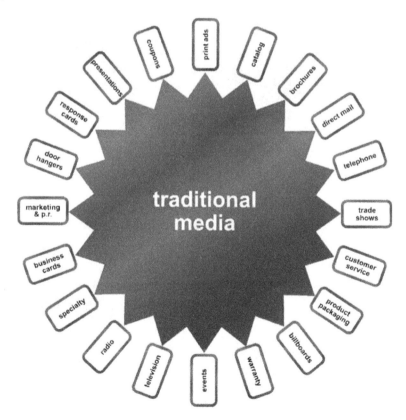

Step 1a - Place Traditional Tools Around Safko Wheel

Select the Traditional Marketing Tools you used last year and any Tools you think you will use this year and remove the remaining Tools from around the Wheel. Your wheel might look something like this Wheel below.

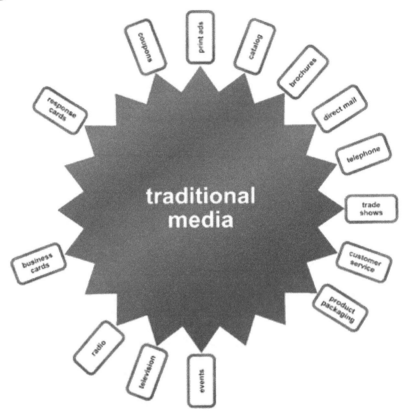

Step 1 b - Remove The Traditional Tools You Didn't Use Last Yearimage56.png

Step 2 – Perform Fusion Marketing (Traditional)

Fusion Marketing is about "fusing" all your marketing Tools together to create a custom master Toolset and discovering new marketing opportunities.

a) Select & Study First Tool
Select one Tool from the Wheel. Study that Tool for a moment to understand how it really works. For example, at first I thought the business card Tool had the worst ROI of any

Tool on the Wheel. I can't remember every making a sale from a business card; however, when I thought about it, I realized that a business card represents a personal relationship. We touched each other (legally), with a handshake. Business cards represent a relationship you can't create through either Traditional or Social Media marketing; it's very personal.

b) Select & Study Your Second Tool
Then, randomly select a second Tool from the Wheel and study it. See what you can find in that Tools that will help you "Fuse" with your prospects and customers. An example would be the coupon Tool. How does my customer use my coupon? What are they thinking? Do they have any questions?

c) The First Fusion Connection

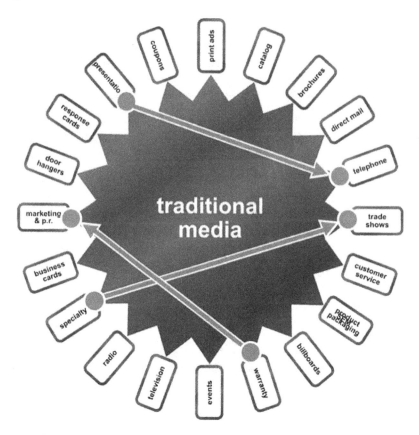

Step 2c - Make Fusion Connections With Random Tools

Now, Fuse Tool 1 with Tool 2. Using the example above How can I Fuse business cards and coupons? Ask yourself "How can they work together?" At first you will not see any logical Connection. It doesn't seem to make sense to Fuse to unrelated Tools. Keep trying, you'll see the Connect ion.

What if you put a coupon on the back of your business card? Nearly everyone's business card is blank on the back. Why? That's important marketing real estate! You would never leave a blank page on a brochure... 10 seconds of dead air on the radio... Then why is your business card back... blank?

We also know that business cards represent a strong interaction, face-to-face, relationship and coupons are a good way to convert a prospect into a customer. Would putting a coupon on your business card make a customer more likely to purchase while holding and viewing your card and remembering meeting and spending time with you? Of course, it would!

Let's look at another Fusion Connection. What if you put the information about your next trade show on the back of your business cards with a QR Barcode that led to a web page or video that said, "If you are in Atlanta on May 23, stop by booth 2103 for a demo and free gift!". Would that generate more traffic? Of course it would.

Business cards are really cheap and now, they are all print on demand. Why not change out your cards every month with the latest promotion on the back of each? If everyone in your company were instructed to hand out business cards to everyone they met, how many cards (promotion pieces), could be handed out each month? And, at the cost of a business card!

d) Reverse Fusion Connections

Now that you can see how to use the Safko Wheel to make one way Fusion Connections from Tool 1 to Tool 2, let's make Reverse Fusion Connections. Start with the first Toolset (Tools 1 and 2) and "Reverse" the Connection to identify additional opportunities. Try it!

What if you Fused the coupon Tool to the business card Tool and put your personal contact information on your coupon, or put a QR Barcode on your coupon that lead to a video of you, reintroducing yourself and asking the card / coupon holder to give you a call? Would that type of personal message increase leads and sales? Yes, it would...

What if you had a real "person", someone that a prospect could speak with, an individual who represented your company with their personal contact information on your coupon? Would that make a prospect more likely to exercise that coupon and convert from a prospect to a customer? Of course it would!

This creates a personal relationship between you and the buyer. Relationships lead to trust. Trust leads to sales. See LinkedIn article "Trust Sells"

e) Multiple Fusion Connections
Now that you have made Connections and Reverse Connections, let's make multiple Fusion Connections. Keep Tool 1, move around the Wheel Fusing that Tool to each, different Tool on the Wheel, one at a time, and discover all the new opportunities hidden in your existing marketing. At first you might not see how they connect, but they will. Give it a chance. Write these ideas down!

f) Reverse New Fusion Connections
Now, reverse each Fusion Connection you make to find more opportunity!

g) Repeat The Fusion Connection Process
When you have completed Fusing your Tool 1 with all of the other Tools, select the another Tool and repeat this whole process again. Move around the Wheel and make Fusion Connections one-way with each new Tool, then reverse each connection!

How many different opportunities can you discover by looking at your Traditional media in this way? The Fusion Marketing way? And, you are already doing it so all these new opportunities came at no extra cost!

Digital Tool Analysis

Step 3 – The Trinity of Social Media

In my books, I talk about The Trinity of Social Media; Blogging, Micro-blogging (Twitter), and Social Networks. With only these three Tools, you can accomplish about 90% of the total success Social Media has to offer.

a) Clear the Wheel and save your chosen Traditional Tool cards aside.
Place the three "Trinity" cards around the Wheel. Add in other Digital / Social Media Marketing Tools that you think are important to your overall marketing strategy; e.g.: SEO (Search Engine Optimization), SEM (Search Engine Marketing), RSS (Really Simple Syndication), Facebook (social networks), You-Tube (video sharing), Email, etc. If you aren't familiar with all

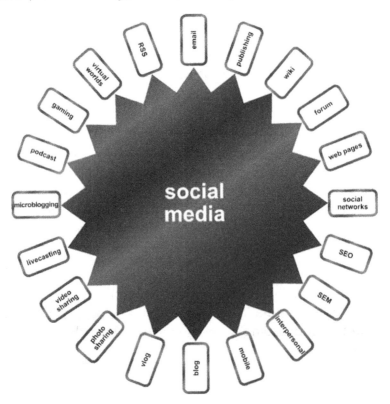

Step 3a - Digital / Social Media Marketing Wheel

20 major Social Media categories, read *The Social Media Bible*.

Step 4 – Perform Digital / Social Fusion Marketing

Refer to Step 2 above and repeat the processes of Fusing all of your Digital / Social Media Tools together to discover even more new opportunities. How many can you identify?

TraDigital Tool Analysis

Step 5 – Create A TraDigital Toolset

Now is the time combine the chosen Traditional Marketing Tools with the chosen Digital / Social Media Marketing Tools by placing them around the Wheel to create one custom, TraDigital Toolset (Traditional + Digital = TraDigital). You can start making all of the Fusion Connections we made above, but...

Step 6 – Perform The Cost of Customer Acquisition (COCA)

You will quickly see that there are just too many possible connections. None of us have the time or resources to pursue all those hidden, but valuable opportunities. With only the 20 Top Traditional and the 20 Top Digital / Social Media Tools, there are 8.15x 10(47)or 8 with 47 zeros after it, combinations. We will have to scale this down somehow that makes sense.

a) To scale this down, we will perform the Cost of Customer Acquisition on each Tool (marketing campaign). Start by listing all of the Traditional campaigns you performed last year on a white-board, yellow-pad, or spreadsheet. List every expense, be sure to include all of your overhead. Total the columns for those expenses. While this should include everyone's hourly wage, payroll burden (usually 32% for vacation, holidays, sick days, and payroll taxes), and other overhead, you can keep it simple if you wish. The more accurate the numbers in, the better the results out.

b) Estimate the number of new customers each campaign generated and write them at the bottom of the campaign columns. Finally, divide the total expense for each of the campaigns by the number of new customers it generated. This is your Cost Of Customer Acquisition, (COCA).

You don't know how many new customers each campaign generated... Then you need to measure! That's another article. If you have been measuring, these numbers will surprise you, some in a good way and some will cause you shock. This is the only step in the Fusion Marketing process that requires a little work. The rest is fun!

Step 7 – Eliminate and Prioritize

a) Here's where you eliminate campaigns that were ineffective; the ones with the poorest ROI or the worst COCA will be

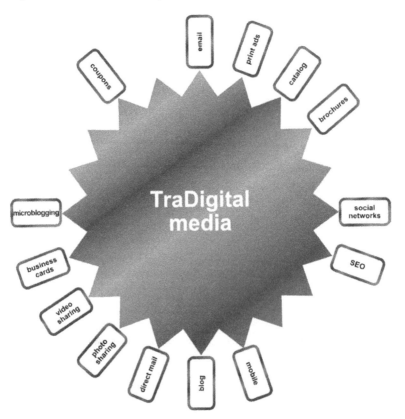

Step 7b - Digital / Social Media TraDigital Marketing Wheelimage

eliminated. Keep doing what's working, stop doing what's not. This will provide new human and financial resources that we can use later on Tools that actually work. Be sure add in any new Tools (cards) you wish to incorporate this year strategy.

I want you to stop doing marketing by accident and begin doing your marketing deliberately.

Fusion Marketing

Step 8 – Perform Fusion Marketing

At this stage, you now have a fully custom set of marketing Tools design by you for you. This process has eliminated all of the Traditional marketing tools you were using, which had little or bad

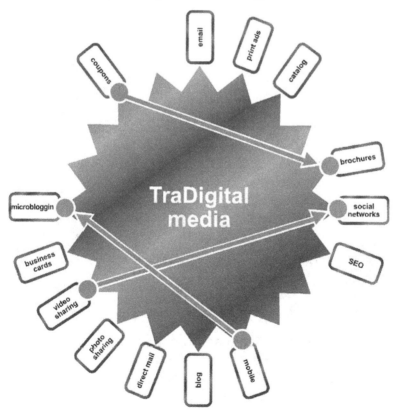

Step 8a - TraDigital Marketing Wheel Connections<No intersecting link>

ROI. You selected Digital / Social Media Tools that you know will work for you and you alone. This TraDigital Toolset is custom designed by you, for your company.

a) Again, refer to Step 2 above for Fusing and Reverse Fusing these Tools and experience the process of Fusing all of your Tools together to discover dozens of new opportunities.

Here is an actual example of what I found when Fusing and Reverse Fusing my custom Tools:

Second Life and Web Pages

I know, I know... Second Life is passé, I get it. It's been dead since 2015; however, we all know that Virtual Reality and Augmented Reality are heading towards marketing at a fierce pace. Where else can you understand these new technologies better? I have more than 1,000 hours logged in to SL. You need to understand it as well!

I chose two random Tools and looked at how they could Connect. I first chose web pages and Second Life (www.SecondLife.com) For those of you who aren't familiar with Second Life, it's an on-line three-dimensional world that people use to meet other people, do business, teach, entertain, and just explore the virtual world. I, like many others, use Second Life for business.

My Second Life Virtual Stores

I have two "real" stores on my virtual property In Second Life where I sell "Three-Dimensional Internet Advertising", which I own three U.S. Patents on and my Educational CD's, DVD, and books. I also hold international meetings and interviews and teach virtual classes for universities around the world. And, I even do Power-Point presentations to groups of avatars (students.)

I chose these two Tools, web sites and Second Life to start with, because I felt that had the lowest ROI and the least in common. Second Life is what they call a "thin client" or small app (software) that runs on your computer and we all know how web pages work.

By using the Safko Wheel and Fusing these two "un-connecta-ble" Tools, I suddenly realized, that on every one of my web sites, any mention of my participation of Second Life, was missing. Nowhere did they say that I am marketing in Second Life. I never would have thought to connect these two unrelated marketing Tools.

VISIT LON IN SECOND LIFE

So, I went to my virtual office in Second Life, grabbed a screen capture of my avatar, and placed the image along with a link back to Second Life on my web sites. Within 24 hours, I saw a 400% increase in my visitors in Second Life! There are 16.5 million members on Second Life, many of whom visit my web sites, but didn't know I was on SL. Now I and driving a significant share of those members from my web site to my virtual store in my virtual world.

The next task was the Fusing the Reverse Connection by promoting my web sites within Second Life. So, I created a large framed image that I placed on the wall in my virtual store that read "Mention Second Life with Your Paid Order And Receive A Free $50 DVD!" Guess what? I saw a 180% increase in traffic in my e-commerce web store in the first 24 hours. This is when I knew Fusion Marketing really works!

Fusing Second Life To My Web Pages
Strategy, Objective, Tool, and Tactic Development

Step 9 – Defining Strategy, Objectives, Tactics, & Tools

In this step I define Strategy, Objectives, Tactics, & Tools and create everything you will need to build a successful Fusion Marketing Plan. Strategy = Objectives + Tools + Tactics.

You might think you know the definition of strategy, but you might not. Go ahead and take a moment to define "strategy" in your head... Really... I'll wait... Not so easy is it?

It's because a Strategy isn't a thing. Strategy is the compilation of your Objectives, Tools, and Tactics. It's an outcome, not a single item. It's like the word "synergy". Synergy is where the whole is greater than the sum of its parts. Stay with me here...

Create Objective

a) Let's begin by creating Objectives, not goals. They're not the same. A goal is a value you place on the outcome of a particular Tactic in order to measure and compare its effectiveness.

We will create 5 Objectives. An Objective is what you want your marketing to accomplish. At the end of the year, quarter, or campaign, what do you want your marketing to achieve, such as; "increase email list", "drive more attendance to presentations", "perform more webinars", or "drive more traffic to my e-commerce store". The "amount" of additional traffic is defined by your goal.

These are the ones I created for my first Fusion Marketing Plan, Create yours and write then down. Create five, no more as you will not have the resources to execute all of the great ideas that you will discover.

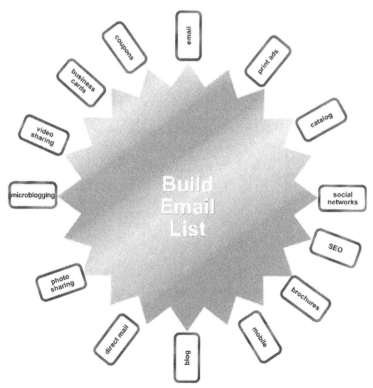

Step 9b - The Safko Strategy Wheel - Objective &Toolsimage

b) Place the first Objective you created in the center of your custom Safko TraDigital Wheel. As an example, I will use "Build Email List", as I know the value of email marketing.

Step 10 – Develop All Of Your Tactics

It's time to work the Wheel now that you have placed one of your Objectives you created in the center of the Wheel.

a) Select each Tool, one at a time, and ask, "How can I use this Tools to achieve that Objective?"
My example question would be, "How can I use 'business cards' to increase my email list?" My answer: "What if I put a QR Barcode on the back of my company cards that lead the holder directly to my email sign up page." Or, "a QR Code to a video explaining the benefits of receiving your emails?" Or, "to

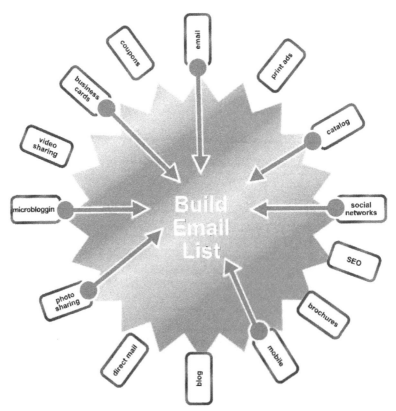

Step 10b - The Safko Strategy Wheel - Objectives, Tools, & Tacticsimage

a web address that offered a white paper or other fish food?" All good ideas? Write them down!

b) Move around the Wheel Fusing each Tool to that one Objective. These Connections are your Tactics. Try making multiple connections; using two or more Tools to Connect to the Objective as in the example above; business cards, QR bar codes, and video sharing. Continue around the Wheel using every Tools. Record every Tactic. Repeat this process with the remaining Objectives until you have fully developed all of the Tactics for all five of your Objectives.

Step 11 – Prioritize Your Tactics

a) The next step is prioritizing each Tactic you recorded for each Objective, because you can't do everything. If you chose only 20 custom Tools and created 5 Objectives, you would discover more than 100 sound executable Tactics that you know will work.

Remember, now that you have performed your COCA in Step 6, and have eliminated Tools (campaigns) with a poor ROI, you now have the human and financial resources, which can be applied to accomplish additional Objectives / Tactics. And you are doing all this anyway so there is no additional expense!

Step 12 – Finalize Your Fusion Marketing Plan

It's the combination all of the above custom Tools generating custom Tactics for each selected custom Objective that becomes your final successful Strategy. This now becomes your new Fusion Marketing Plan!

By utilizing Fusion Marketing and the Safko Wheel process you will only spend resources on implementing your most effective Tactics, on the most effective Objectives, using the most effective Traditional Marketing Tools, combined with the most effective Digital Marketing Tools, to develop the most effective Strategy!

That's it! Fusion Marketing is a process that systematically encourages you to look at all of your marketing in a completely different way to identify hidden opportunities to increase your ROI without spending any additional money.

Isn't this every marketer's dream? To see greater ROI across every category of marketing with less cost?

EXECUTE WITH SUCCESS!

Fusion and the Safko Wheel can take your marketing into other dimensions. With the Safko Wheel, you can drill down and validate every Tools you choose. This process is called "Fractal Fusion". The next article will explain Fractal Fusion!

About Lon Safko

Lon Safko is an innovator, inventor, best-selling author, speaker, trainer, consultant, and is the creator of the "First Computer To Save A Human Life" as coined by Steve Jobs, Apple, Inc. That computer, along with 18 of Lon's inventions are part of the permanent collection of the Smithsonian Institution in Washington, D.C. along with 30,000 of Lon's personal papers along with 14 inventions in the collection of The Computer History Museum in Mountainview, CA.

Lon hosted the first ever PBS Television Special "Social Media & You... Communicating In A Digital World".

Lon developed the world's first "voice recognition", "voice synthesizing" and pioneered home automation, all done with the physically challenged in mind. Lon is also the designer the archetypes for the Apple Newton world first PDA, & Microsoft's "Bob" operating system and those handy little "Tool-Tips" help-balloon pop-ups!

Lon holds three United States Patents and is a 2017 Pulitzer Prize Nominee and author of multiple innovative best-selling books *The Social Media Bible*, published by John Wiley & Sons, now in its Third Edition and five languages and hitting #1 on Amazon is the most comprehensive book on social media marketing ever written and just broke the $2m retail sales mark.

Lon's newest best-seller *The Fusion Marketing Bible*, published by McGraw Hill is already in three languages and hit #3 on Amazon will change the way the world will be doing marketing in 2020.

Lon is also a renowned international speaker, and trainer, teaching the world's largest companies how to harness innovative thinking, social media, and digital communications strategies, to create higher productivity and profits.

Connect with the Authors

Ian Cleary *razorsocial.com*
Andrea Vahl *andreavahl.com*
Dave Kerpen *hdavekerpen.ceo*
Phyllis Khare *phylliskhare.com*
Brian Massey *conversionsciences.com/blog/author/bmassey*
Emeric Ernoult *twitter.com/eernoult*
Erik Qualman *equalman.com*
Jamie Turner *60secondmarketer.com*
John Jantsch *johnjantsch.com*
Martin Shervington *martinshervington.com*
Viveka von Rosen *linkedintobusiness.com*
Michael Brenner *marketinginsidergroup.com*
Andrew Davis *www.akadrewdavis.com*
Lon Safko *www.lonsafko.com*

CPSIA information can be obtained
at www.ICGtesting.com
Printed in the USA
BVHW041657230922
647859BV00013B/178